OXFORD ENGLISH FOR CAREERS

TOURISM

Robin Walker and Keith Harding

Teacher's Resource Book

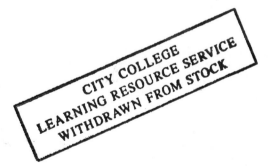

OXFO
UNIVERSITY

OXFORD
UNIVERSITY PRESS

Great Clarendon Street, Oxford OX2 6DP

Oxford University Press is a department of the University of Oxford.
It furthers the University's objective of excellence in research, scholarship,
and education by publishing worldwide in

Oxford New York

Auckland Cape Town Dar es Salaam Hong Kong Karachi
Kuala Lumpur Madrid Melbourne Mexico City Nairobi
New Delhi Shanghai Taipei Toronto

With offices in

Argentina Austria Brazil Chile Czech Republic France Greece
Guatemala Hungary Italy Japan Poland Portugal Singapore
South Korea Switzerland Thailand Turkey Ukraine Vietnam

OXFORD and OXFORD ENGLISH are registered trade marks of
Oxford University Press in the UK and in certain other countries

ACKNOWLEDGEMENTS

The authors and publisher are grateful to the following for their permission
to reproduce photographs and illustrative material:

Getty Images cover (Deborah Jaffe / Taxi), pp.70 (Jerry Driendl /
Photographer's Choice), 72 (Peter Adams / Image Bank), 86 (Stephanie
Rausser / Taxi), 88 (Fergus O'Brien / Taxi); Punchstock p.84 (Photodisc).

Illustrations by:
Pierre d'Alancaisez pp.71, 74;
David Atkinson / NB Illustration p.19;
Tim Kahane pp.75, 79, 80, 81, 83, 90;
Stephanie Wunderlich / Three in a Box p77.

Contents

Introduction

Tourism is divided into three levels. Level 1 (Provision) deals with the areas of tourism related to the creation, promotion and selling of typical tourism products such as flights and package holidays. Level 2 (Encounters) presents students with the English needed to handle face-to-face contact with tourists who are on holiday. Level 3 (Management) covers the language needed for discussion of tourism issues at basic managerial level.

Take off

This is designed as a warm-up activity to the unit. It often introduces key vocabulary or concepts, and should be used to get students to focus on the topic.

Also, try bringing in your own pictures (e.g. in Unit 2, a photo of you at a famous attraction or destination). Students enjoy this type of teacher personalization, and you can encourage them to do the same.

It's my job / Where in the world?

These occur in alternate units, and provide visual input and text. They are all based on authentic interviews and sources and are designed to be of interest to the students as they stand with only minimal tasks. In 'It's my job', students will read about a variety of young people in different tourism environments and gain insight into the skills required.

General focus questions for 'It's my job' and 'Where in the world?' are: *What do you think his / her job involves? Would you like to do it? Where do you think this is? What do you know about it?*

As an ongoing project, encourage the class to build up a portfolio of other 'It's my job' or 'Where in the world?' features.

Customer care

This is a very important part of the tourism industry. All the Customer care sections have a cartoon designed to make the point in an interesting or amusing way. This is a good starting point for the teacher, and it also helps if you can add other examples, especially authentic ones from your own experience.

Taken together, the twelve sections form a useful training manual for Customer care, which can be related directly to specific jobs in tourism.

Find out

This encourages students to take an active role in the learning process, both in terms of their English language work and the subject of tourism itself.

Activities can be set as projects or homework assignments, but it is worth spending time in class preparing students for the task. Help can also be given by brainstorming some standard places and sites where they can gather information.

Also, make sure students know how to do internet searches using search engines such as www.google.com or www.altavista.com. If students get stuck, www.tourist-offices.org.uk and www.unwto.org are also extremely useful tourism-specific sites.

Top margin

This top part of the page contains facts, statistics, and quotes. These are optional extras and can be used to add variety and interest to your lessons, or provide additional material for strong students who are 'fast finishers'.

Sometimes they have an associated question, and ways of exploitation include asking whether your students are surprised by the facts and statistics, or whether they agree, disagree, or can identify with the quotes.

There are also definitions for difficult words or phrases which are important to understand a text which appears on the same page. (The words or phrases in the text are highlighted in **bold**.)

Vocabulary

Students meet a large amount of vocabulary during the course. It is important to encourage good learning skills from the start, for example:

- organizing vocabulary into categories rather than simple alphabetical lists
- understanding the context of vocabulary and whether it is a key word needed for production or for comprehension
- checking and learning the pronunciation of a word or phrase.

All of these learner skills are brought together in the Personal Learning Dictionary (PLD) established in Unit 1, (see the teaching notes).

Language spot

This focuses on the grammar that is generated by the topic of the unit and concentrates on its practical application.

If your students need revision after completing the Language spot, direct them to the Grammar reference, which provides a handy check.

There is also one photocopiable Grammar test for each unit in this Teacher's Resource Book.

Listening, Reading, Speaking, Writing

These activities give realistic and communicative practice of language skills needed in tourism.
● In the listening activities students are exposed to industry situations, including dialogues, presentations, and interviews. They also hear a variety of English accents, both native-speaker and non-native speaker.
● In the reading sections students meet a variety of industry-based texts. These cover basic tourism concepts that they may be familiar with already from other tourism subjects they are studying.
● In the speaking sections, try to ensure use of English during speaking activities, particularly those involving some discussion. Encourage this by teaching or revising any functional language students may need. There is also one photocopiable Communication activity for each unit in this Teacher's Resource Book.
● Writing practice in the units is consolidation of the topic with structured, meaningful writing tasks (see Writing bank).

Pronunciation

This practises aspects of pronunciation which are of maximum importance for intelligibility.

You can repeat the recordings in the Pronunciation as often as you like until you and your students to feel confident they have mastered a particular sound or feature.

Checklist

This allows students to check their own progress. You may want to get students to grade or assess how well they can perform each of the 'Can do' statements, e.g. 'easily', 'with difficulty', or 'not at all'.

Key words

These are the main items of tourism vocabulary introduced in the unit. A definition of each of these words appears in the Glossary. Students may want to transfer some of the words to their PLD (see Vocabulary). You should certainly check students' pronunciation, including the stress, of words likely to be used orally.

Next stop

This introduces the topic of the following unit. Students can discuss the questions in pairs or small groups to exchange information on their experiences. Mostly, the questions will put the students in the position of tourists and users of tourism products, rather than tourism providers.

Writing bank

This is in the middle of the book and gives more in-depth skills practice in basic writing for tourism. It can be used throughout the course, either in class, or as self-study or homework. There are recommendations for when to use the different exercises in the teaching notes in this Teacher's Resource Book. There is also an Answer key in the Student's Book to encourage students to check their work, but it is important for you to check extended written answers with reference to the models provided.

Pairwork

This section contains one or more parts of the information gap activities from the main units (see Speaking).

Grammar reference

This can be used together with the Language spot, as a handy check or revision. It shows the form of a particular grammar point, briefly explains its use, and provides example sentences as well as indicating likely student errors.

Listening scripts

This is a complete transcript of all the recordings. Direct students to it for checking answers after they have completed a listening task, or allow weaker students to read it as they listen to a particular recording, perhaps for a final time.

Glossary

This is an alphabetical list of all the Key words. Each word is followed by the pronunciation in phonetic script, the part of speech, and a definition in English.

The section begins with a phonetic chart, with an example word from tourism to illustrate each of the sounds.

1 What is tourism?

Background

Because we are all tourists, the English of tourism feels familiar. However, it is a complex activity. For the *World Tourism Organization* (www.unwto.org), a specialized agency of the United Nations:

'Tourism comprises the activities of persons travelling to and staying in places outside their usual environment for not more than one consecutive year for leisure, business, and other purposes not related to the exercise of an activity remunerated from within the place visited.'

The WTO employs three key criteria to determine if a trip is tourism: *displacement*, *purpose*, and *duration*.

- *Displacement* is the most important. Normally transport is involved, but displacement by bicycle, horse, or on foot is also included.

- The key to *purpose* is that you are not going to receive payment for the activity you carry out from people or organizations in the region you travel to.
- The last of the criteria refers to a *maximum stay*, which for the WTO is one year. The WTO doesn't set a minimum – day-trippers are clearly tourists.

Tourism lies at the centre of a matrix of industries.

The tourism industry gives rise to many jobs that involve a wide range of personal qualities, skills, and knowledge. This is one of the most attractive aspects of the industry, and students beginning a diploma or degree in tourism are almost guaranteed to find a job that suits their personality perfectly.

➕ Additional activity

(all levels)
To help the students gel and to give further practice of jobs vocabulary (including *What do you do?*):
- Give each student a piece of paper with a short sentence for each of the jobs (e.g. *I fly planes, I sell holidays*).
- Get the students to mingle and have the following dialogue:
  - A *Hello, my name's X. What's yours?*
  - B *Y. What do you do?*
  - A *I fly planes.*
  - B *So you're a pilot.*
  - A *That's right. What about you?*, etc.

✱ Tip

Opposites – *calm* and *nervous*

Adjectives do not always have absolute opposites. *Nervous* in English usually means anxious or worried about something that is about to happen or is happening. In this sense the opposite is *calm*. Give students some example situations to illustrate *nervous*, e.g. just before an exam or a visit to the dentist or when the boss is visiting.

Take off

- Students work in pairs or small groups on **1** to **3**, then report back to the whole class. **4** can be done in open class.

> **1** a pilot   c resort rep   e travel agent
>   b tour guide   d flight attendant   f receptionist
> **2 Possible answers**
> Travel jobs: pilot, flight attendant, airline check-in clerk, (porter)
> Hotel jobs: receptionist, waiter, chef, porter, hotel manager
> Tourist attractions: tour guide, tourist information officer, resort rep
> Retail jobs: travel agent

Vocabulary

Adjectives for job skills

- Demonstrate one 'easy' pair of adjectives (e.g. *friendly – unfriendly*). Pairs do **1**, using dictionaries if possible, and report back. Pay attention to pronunciation. Note that there are not direct pairings for all the adjectives. **2** can be done in pairs, then discussed in groups, before class feedback.

> **1** calm – nervous, extrovert – shy, friendly – unfriendly, hardworking – lazy, organized – disorganized, smart – scruffy

Speaking
Careers questionnaire

- Students do **1** on their own, then **2** in pairs. **3** can be discussed in open class.

Language spot
Describing job skills

- Write three of the sentences on the board:

  *I enjoy **meeting** new people.*   *I can **make** people relax.*
  *I know how **to use** computers.*

- Focus on the gerund, and infinitive with or without *to*.

- Ask students to find other examples of the gerund and infinitive (with or without *to*) in the Careers Questionnaire in *Speaking*.

- Focus on the use of *have to* (and third person *has to*) before or after students complete **1**. They will need to be able to use it for **2**.

🔑
1 1 working   4 speak   7 use
     2 work   5 understanding   8 work
     3 smile   6 using   9 working / being

It's my job

- Ask general questions about the photo – *Where is it? Would you like to go there?* Then ask students to answer the questions in pairs and report back.

🔑
   1 when he was 12
   2 restaurant assistant, chef, hotel front desk, car rental supervisor, hotel night manager, airline check-in clerk
   3 runs his own tour company (tour operator)
   4 you've got to love your work and love people
   5 to become Minister of Tourism or Director of Tourism for Jamaica

Listening
Three jobs

- 🎧 Use the photos to set the scene. Pre-teach *day off, shifts, back office* in **1**. Listen again for **2**. Check answers in pairs, then whole class.

> **1** 1 Kelly: receptionist, John: tourist information office manager, Suzanna: resort rep
> 2 a Kelly and Suzanna b Suzanna c Kelly d John e Suzanna
>
> **2** 1 check in   8 don't deal   14 arrange
> 2 room keys   9 email   15 'm working
> 3 reservations   10 start   16 long hours
> 4 shifts   11 email   17 guests
> 5 usually   12 sets   18 problems
> 6 occasionally   13 we're providing 19 often don't finish
> 7 'm doing

Language spot
Describing job routines

- Look at the example and identify the different tenses and their uses.
- Students do **2** in pairs and report back, then do **3** individually or in pairs.

> **1** I start = habitual action (Present Simple), I'm doing = temporary activity (Present Continuous)
> **2** **Extract 1** check in, hand out, process, work, start, is, get off, do, don't finish, 'm doing
> **Extract 2** don't deal, 'm, start, sets, have to, 're providing, want, 're stocking, arrange, get, 'm working
> **Extract 3** work, take, are going, bring back, have to, are, don't finish
> **3** 1 finish, 'm working   4 'm waiting, wants, 're thinking
> 2 don't have, is taking place 5 work, 'm doing, go / 'm going
> 3 don't have, are you staying

Top margin

- Write *Tourism is ...* on the board. Ask students to add possible endings.
- Ask if students agree with the first definition. Discuss what *temporary short-term* means. Ask if they agree that tourism has changed the world. How?

Speaking
Job skills

- Get students to write the questions in **1** first, before starting **2**. After **2**, students can look at each other's tables to check their answers.

➕ Additional activity
(stronger students)
The extracts contain a number of phrasal verbs. Give the students an example – *check in*. Then explain what phrasal verbs are if they don't already know (a verb with a preposition or adverb to create a different meaning), and ask them to find five more examples in the extracts.

➕ Additional activity
(stronger students)
Get students to use the chart to ask other people they know about their jobs (preferably people working in tourism). They will need to convert the questions to the second person. The information they find out can be used to build their own file or portfolio of tourism professionals.

1 How old is he / she?

What does he / she do?

What qualities and skills does he / she have?

What hours does he / she work?

What are his / her typical daily tasks?

What does he / she enjoy about his / her job?

How does he / she relax after work?

How does he / she spend his / her own holidays?

+ Additional activity

(all levels)

Ask the students to match the jobs from *Take off* with the different sectors.

Vocabulary

Industry sectors

● Refer back to the categories that students came up with in *Take off* **2**. Compare with the hexagon. Do **1** and **2** in pairs and then report back to whole class. **2** will be developed more in *Find out* and *Writing*.

1 a tour operators d transport

b accommodation and catering e public sector tourism

c tourist attractions f retail (travel agents and online)

Pronunciation

● Check students understand *syllable* and *strongest*. You may like to introduce the word *stressed* as a more correct word for *strongest*.

● 🎧 In **2**, ask students to guess the number of syllables before listening.

1 and **2**

	Number of syllables			Strongest
Word	1	2	3	
attendant			✓	second
manager			✓	first
catering			✓	first
guide	✓			—
porter		✓		first
tourism			✓	first
pilot		✓		first
attractions			✓	second
calm	✓			—

+ Additional activity

(stronger students)

For more advanced students – or students who have plenty of ideas – get them to modify the *It's about ...* statements and / or produce some statements of their own.

Customer care

'The customer is always right'

● Use the cartoon to generate discussion about **1**. In case discussion is not forthcoming, have some situations ready, for example:

A hotel guest who wants to change room because it overlooks a building site.

A hotel guest who wants the restaurant to close earlier because he likes to go to bed at 9 p.m. and it is too noisy.

● Ask students (in pairs) to produce their own, to be discussed in class. For **2**, start by giving some examples of your own.

Find out

- Students should store the sources of information (websites, addresses of national tourist offices, etc.) as they will need them in many of the *Find out* sections throughout the course. This activity leads directly into *Writing*.

Writing
Country fact sheet

- In pairs or small groups, students share their information from *Find out* and complete the fact sheet, which will be a useful reference document later.

Reading
Tourism: the biggest business in the world

- Ask some general questions related to the topic of the article:

  How important is tourism to your country?
  Name one important development in tourism in the last 50 years.
  What difficulties (or 'challenges') are there for the tourism industry today?

- Students do **1** in pairs. Read (**2**) to check and report back. Then pairs work through **3** and report back.

> **⊙—**
> **1** 1 F   2 T   3 T   4 F
> **3** 1 a the year in which Thomas Cook organized his first excursion
>   b the number of international tourist arrivals in 1950
>   c the number of international tourist arrivals in 2004
>   d the estimated number of international tourist arrivals in 2020
>   2 Positive: it creates many good jobs and careers, it can help to protect environments and animal life, it can save cultures and the local way of life, it can change countries and people for the better
>   Negative: it produces many poor and badly paid jobs, it can damage environments and animal life, it can destroy cultures and the local way of life, it can change countries and people for the worse

Vocabulary
Personal Learning Dictionaries (PLD)

- Use **2** to show that students can add information to this and, more importantly, personalize their PLD entries (e.g. give example sentences from class or their own experience, which will be more memorable).

- Make sure that students understand that the PLD will be ongoing through the course, and that they should have a suitable file or book.

> **⊙—**
> **1** Five: spelling, pronunciation, part of speech, countable / uncountable, definition
> **2** translation in your language, use in an example sentence, related words

Checklist, Key words, Next stop

See suggestions on p.5. Remind students about transferring vocabulary into their Personal Learning Dictionaries.

✷ Tip
Varieties of text
Explain that 'writing' is not always sentence-based. Texts like this, as well as other charts and graphs, focus on ideas and points. They are often the types of text that students of tourism will encounter and need to produce in the profession.

➕ Additional activity
(all levels)
Question 3 in **3** can be done as a class game, going round the class giving one job each in alphabetical order, with students dropping out when they meet a letter for which they can't find a job. Any job can count if the student can justify its relevance to tourism (even X-ray machine operator – the person who operates the luggage X-ray security machine).

✷ Tip
Specialist dictionaries
As well as ordinary dictionaries, there are a number of specialist dictionaries which your students (or institution) can buy:
- Oxford Business English Dictionary
- Dictionary of Hotels, Tourism and Catering Management (PH Collin, Peter Collin Publishing)
- Complete A–Z Travel and Leisure Handbook (R Youell, Hodder Education)
- The website www.lexicool.com has online bilingual dictionaries of tourism.

2 World destinations

Background

Destinations can be cities, towns, natural regions, or even whole countries. The economies of all tourist destinations are dependent to a significant extent on the money produced by tourism.

It is possible to classify destinations as natural or built:

- *Natural destinations* include seas, lakes, rivers, coasts, mountain ranges, deserts, and so on.
- *Built destinations* are cities, towns, and villages.
- A *resort* is a destination constructed mainly or completely to serve the needs of tourism, such as Cancun in Mexico.

Mass-market destinations, like Benidorm in Spain, receive millions of tourists every year. *Upmarket* destinations like the Seychelles offer greater quality at higher prices for fewer visitors. Destinations that only appeal to very specific groups of tourists are known as *niche market* destinations.

Successful destinations are seen to be unique in some way by those who visit them. *Climate* is one of the features that determines this uniqueness. Not surprisingly, *temperate* and *tropical* climates attract the greatest numbers of visitors. *Location* affects destinations in terms of *accessibility*. Places that are easy to get to receive more visitors.

All destinations contain *attractions*. Thus, London is a tourist destination, but the Tower of London is a tourist attraction. *Natural attractions* include forests, national parks, waterfalls, canyons, and so on. *Built attractions* like the Taj Mahal or the Pyramids are historical attractions. These are very different from *purpose-built attractions* like theme parks, because their original function was not tourism.

The movement of people to and from tourist destinations produces *tourism flows*:

- *Domestic tourism* occurs when tourists visit destinations in their own country.
- People travelling to destinations in a different country are participating in *outbound tourism*.
- *Inbound (incoming) tourism* involves people arriving in a destination from another country.

Some countries create more tourism than others. The main *tourism generators* in the world today are Germany, the USA, the UK, Italy, Canada, and France. In 2001 they were responsible for 40% of all international travel. The top four destinations are currently France, the USA, Spain, and Italy. Tourists from economically strong nations spend a lot of money, making these countries the top *tourism spenders*. The countries that receive the most *revenue* from tourism, the USA, Spain, France, and Italy, are the top *tourism earners*.

✚ Additional activity

(all levels)

Start to build up a collection of pictures of famous attractions – postcards, magazine pictures, your own photographs. These can be used for various activities throughout the course, but here you can use them to give more practice of the vocabulary categories for tourist attractions and the names of countries. You do not need to do this at this stage, but could do it as a warmer for another lesson from this unit.

You can also use the cards for other speaking practice – e.g. students in groups decide on an order in which they would most like to visit the attractions.

Take off

- Focus attention on the photos and maps, and identify one in open class as an example, e.g. *Summer Palace, Beijing – palace – China*.

- Students work in pairs or small groups on **1** to **3** and then check answers with the whole class. **4** can be done in open class.

🔑
  a Mount Etna – natural geographic feature – Italy (map 2)
  b Neuschwanstein Castle – castle – Germany (map 5)
  c Disneyland – theme park – USA (map 1)
  d St Basil's Cathedral – cathedral – Russia (map 6)
  e Copacabana Beach – beach – Brazil (map 3)
  f Summer Palace, Beijing – palace – China (map 4)

∗ Tip
Phonetic labelling
Label some of the countries and cities on the class world map with their phonetic transcription. If you have other display space, put up flags of some of the countries and label them with the transcription. You can do the same with the pictures and postcards suggested in *Take off*. Having transcriptions around the room in this way will familiarize the students with IPA.

Pronunciation

- Most students are not confident at using the IPA transcription. The purpose here is to build up their confidence to use the IPA to help them pronounce words. Discuss the practical value of being able to use the IPA transcriptions in dictionaries. Do the first two identifications in **1** in open class.

- 🎧 Students work through the other activities, checking answers and practising in pairs where appropriate.

> **⚷**
> **2**
> | Spain | Russia | Madrid |
> | France | Canada | Paris |
> | London | Italy | Hungary |
> | Mexico | Moscow | Tokyo |
> | China | Athens | Germany |
> | Rome | Japan | Brazil |
>
> **3**
> | Russia | Madrid | France | Paris | London | Italy |
> | Mexico | Tokyo | China | Japan | | |
>
> **6** The stress marker (') appears before the stressed syllable.

Listening
Where do tourists go?

- In **1**, ask for examples of *domestic, inbound,* and *outbound* tourism. Encourage guesswork for **2**, and correct pronunciation if necessary.

- 🎧 For **4**, practise the vowel sounds /i/ and /iː/ and stress shift in 'ninety / nine'teen. Ensure students can recognize the difference, and produce it.

> **⚷**
> **1** 1 b   2 c   3 a
> **3** a 19,000   b 80 million   c 30.5   d 15
> **6** 1 France 75m, 2 USA 51m, 3 Spain 48m, 4 Italy 41m, 5 China 31m,
>   6 UK 25m, 7= Mexico and Russia 21m, 9 Canada 20m, 10 Germany 19m

Top margin

- Ask students to guess how many tourists travel internationally every year, and where they come from. They can also guess the ratio of Japanese and American tourists to Hawaiians in Hawaii in the summer.

- Let them read the facts to check their guesses. How close were they?

∗ Tip
Statistical reliability
Note that statistics for the generation of tourists can be unreliable, because it is very difficult to differentiate tourists from other travellers and forms of migration. The high position of Poland, the Czech Republic, and Malaysia in this data may be a result of this – and it is this that may surprise students (in **3**).

Reading
Where do tourists come from?

- Encourage students to speculate in **1**, and, for **2**, which countries the flags represent. The speculation will give you an opportunity to work on pronunciation of other countries.

> **O—**
> **2** 1 Germany 73m, 2 USA 58m, 3 Poland 55m, 4 UK 54m, 5 Czech
> Republic 40m, 6 Malaysia 26m, 7 Italy 19m, 8= Canada and Russia 18m,
> 10 France 17m, 11 Japan 16m.

Speaking
The biggest spenders and the biggest earners

● Ask students to study the word grid and then answer **1** and **2** in pairs.

● Work in different pairs for **3**. Do not let students look at each other's work until **4**.

> **O—**
> **1** 1 spend, earn, earn, spend   3 expenses, receipt
>   2 earners, earnings, earn   4 expenditure, receipts

✱ Tip

heritage

The concept of *heritage* may be a difficult one for students to grasp (and it doesn't fit easily into the categories in **1**). But it is an important one in tourism and it is worth spending some time on it. It can be defined as 'the traditions, qualities, and culture of a country that have existed for a long time and that have great importance for the country'. Write this definition on the board and help your students to think of actual examples of heritage in their own country.

Vocabulary
Tourism features and attractions

● This activity encourages students to store and learn vocabulary in categories. They can use the chart in the book or copy it into their own notes – it will be a valuable resource. Ensure also that they are aware of the pronunciation of the words they record, e.g. you can ask them to mark the stress.

● If you have been building a picture library in the class, you can use this as a resource for more vocabulary for **3**.

● For **4**, students take turns to make a sentence using a different word from the chart each time.

> **O—**
> **1**
> Climate: chilly, temperate, damp
> Natural features: harbour, waterfall, countryside, heritage, coastline
> Built attractions: castle, heritage
> Events: music festival, concert
> Food, drink, and entertainment: music festival, concert, art gallery, nightlife
> Accommodation: campsite
> Transport: harbour, metro
> **2** 1 countryside   2 coastline   3 temperate   4 heritage

Customer care
Different destinations – different customs

● The main aim here is to develop a basic sense of cultural awareness. It's a good idea to start with the students' personal experience. Ask students for any information on different cultures they have encountered.

● Get students to relate the subject matter to specific situations, e.g. *greetings, ordering food, queuing,* etc.

Where in the world?

- Write column headings on the board (*climate, geography / location, natural features, main attractions, importance*). Get students to brainstorm what they know about New Zealand and the Balearic Islands, with you writing information in the appropriate column. At this stage don't confirm or reject anything, as this will set an automatic focus task for reading the texts.

- Use the pictures to stimulate ideas for the brainstorming, and pre-teach some of the more unusual vocabulary, e.g. *bungee-jumping, olive grove*.

Oⁿ
3 New Zealand = reference book, Balearic Islands = advertisement or brochure

* Tip

Genre

This *Language spot* not only focuses on the function of 'describing resources and features', it also introduces students to the idea of genre in tourism texts. Genre analysis is an important part of ESP, and work on it should begin early. Here students will be asked to identify and then produce the features of two genres in a simple genre-switching exercise: factual reference descriptions, and brochure advertising descriptions.

Language spot
Describing resources and features

- Do **1**, **2**, and **3** in open class, writing the expressions in **2** on the board.
- **4** and **5** can be done in pairs with a reporting back stage after each activity. Pay careful attention to error and appropriate genre in these activities, and make sure you have a clear correction stage.

Oⁿ
1 No, it doesn't.
2 **Floating** between Spain and the North African coast, the Balearic Islands **offer** the perfect location for a fantastic holiday. There are four main islands for you to **choose** from ...
The gorgeous climate **boasts** more than 300 days a year of guaranteed sunshine ... The long hot summer **stretches** from May to October... Sun-seekers will **love** the fabulous beaches. Fun-seekers will **enjoy** the exciting nightlife – the clubs and discos of Ibiza **provide** plenty of entertainment for young people.
3 There are four main islands for you to choose from ... You can also enjoy wonderful architecture ... You can take a relaxing fishing or sailing trip ... If you go in June, don't miss the spectacular Fiesta of San Juan ... Whatever you want from a holiday, the Balearics will help you find it.
4 **Possible answer** There are two islands for you to choose from, each with its own attractions. The varied climate stretches from subtropical in the north to very cold in the south. New Zealand boasts some fascinating scenery. Walkers and mountain climbers will enjoy the mountains and lakes. Adventure-seekers will love activities like bungee-jumping. You can also enjoy attractions such as the Maori culture. You can take an interesting trip fishing or whale-watching.

> If you are a fan of films, you can visit some of the places where *Lord of the Rings* was filmed.
> **5 Possible answer** The Balearic Islands consist of four main islands. The climate is hot and sunny with temperatures around 27 °C during the summer. The main attractions for tourists are the beaches, and there is plenty of entertainment and nightlife. Other attractions include architecture, hilltop villages, olive groves, and fishing and sailing trips. There are also a number of festivals.

Listening
Favourite places

- 🎧 Look at the pictures and practise describing location (especially the vocabulary that occurs in the listening scripts) before listening. Use **3** and **4** to point out that collocation is a useful way of remembering vocabulary.

> 🔑
>
> **1** a Scotland   b Barcelona   c Ibiza
> **2** a it's remote and an escape, views, walking   c nightlife and bars
>   b architecture, food, happy memories
> **3** remote cottage, spectacular views, ruined castle, dramatic coastline
>   (You can also say *spectacular coastline*.)
> **4** In the listening script: cheap flights, cultural heritage, delicious food, happy memories, relaxing break, exciting nightlife, lively bars, crowded beaches
>   (Other possible word combinations: cheap bars, cheap food, exciting bars, lively nightlife, crowded bars)

Speaking
Describing a destination

- Give the students time to prepare their statements in **1**. While monitoring you can award extra points for using the target language effectively.

- **2** sets the scene for *Writing* (you can use a board grid as suggested earlier for New Zealand and the Balearic Islands).

Writing
Describing a destination

- Set the writing either as a class activity or for homework.

➕ Additional activity
(all levels)
You can get some extra genre practice by getting students to swap their completed descriptions with a partner who must then rewrite in the alternative genre.

Find out

- Brainstorm information sources, referring back to *Find out* in Unit 1. For students who are studying in their own country and do not have much experience of other places, get them to choose one of the topic areas in **1**.

Checklist, Key words, Next stop

See suggestions on p.5. Remind students about transferring vocabulary into their Personal Learning Dictionaries.

3 Tour operators

Background

Tour operators bring together transport, transfers, accommodation, meals, attractions, and other services to make a *package holiday*. This is the same as a *package tour* and the names reflect the fact that for a fixed price the customer buys all of the main components of their holiday.

The main advantages of package holidays are:

- They are cheaper than if you buy each component separately.
- Customers know how much their holiday will cost before leaving home.
- Customers do not have to spend time buying each component separately.
- The standard of the transport, accommodation, and services has been checked by professionals.
- There will a *representative* (rep) at the destination.

Tour operators buy the components from the *principals* – the airlines, hotel companies, and so on. By buying *in bulk*, tour operators can negotiate much lower prices than those an individual member of the public would obtain. Companies that buy in large quantities and sell to make a profit are called *wholesalers*.

Tour operators form part of the *chain of distribution*, and act as the link between the principals and the travel agents. However, tour operators can sell directly to tourists via the Internet. In addition, individual tourists can buy directly from the principals and get even better prices. Low-cost airlines work like this.

There are four types of tour operator:

- *Mass market tour operators* like TUI and Thomas Cook create package holidays for people travelling to the world's most popular and most economical destinations.
- *Domestic tour operators* specialize in packages for people travelling inside their own country.
- *Inbound tour operators* produce packages for tourists coming into a country from abroad.
- *Specialist tour operators* offer packages to people with specific interests such as sailing or climbing.

Some of the world's bigger tour operators form part of companies that own their own aircraft, hotels, ancillary services, and travel agencies. These companies participate in each step in the chain, and compete directly with travel agencies on the one hand, or with the principals on the other. The German group TUI AG, currently the world's largest travel group, has over 250 hotels, five airlines, and tour operations in sixteen countries.

Tour operation is a risky business. Fashions change, and political instability, terrorism, or natural disasters can alter demand. Unlike a television, a holiday cannot be stored until the market is ready for it again. Tourism products are described as *perishable*. If they are not sold by a specific date, they are lost altogether. 50 seats on a plane to the Seychelles for 2 May have no value at all on 3 May.

Take off

- Bring in some examples of holiday brochures, ideally in English. Get students to look at the pictures, and any brochures you have brought in. Ask the students what they all have in common and then teach the term *package holiday*, and look at the dictionary extract.

- Students do **1** to **4** in pairs and then report back.

  1 traditional sun, sea, and sand holiday, safari, skiing, cultural tour

Listening

Why choose a package holiday?

- 🎧 Get students to predict possible answers before they listen. (For **1** they have already done this in *Take off* **4**.)

● Students can check answers in pairs before reporting back.

> **⚬┳**
>
> **1** cheaper; you know how much it's going to cost; organized by professionals; tour rep available on site to help with problems
> **2** 1 c   2 a,b
> **3** deals with problems on site
> **4** you can relax knowing someone will help you if you have a problem

✚ Additional activity

(stronger students)
If you work in an area where there are local English-speaking tour operators (or travel agents), then this would be a good opportunity to invite them along to give a talk. The questions listed later in *Find out* could then be asked directly to the speaker. Make sure that students visit the website of the tour operator first, so that they can listen from an informed perspective.

Reading
The role of tour operators

● Ask students if they know what a tour operator does. Get them to name tour operators in their country.

● This is quite a lengthy reading, so focus on the diagram first to establish the basic flow and organization. Remind students that they do not need to understand every word of the text. You may also want to treat the text in two halves, breaking after the second paragraph (i.e. up to ... *by other systems*).

● Pairs compare answers before reporting back. If you are dividing the text in two, then compare and report back on 1 to 3, then 4 to 6.

> **⚬┳**
>
> **1** a transport to and from the destination, transfers between the airport / station / port and accommodation, food and accommodation at the destination, services of guide or rep
>   b travel agent
>   c four: mass market operators, specialist operators, domestic operators, incoming tour operators
> **2** package tour, inclusive tour (IT)
> **3** b
> **4** to get a cheaper price (economies of scale)
> **5** they don't have to pay commission to a travel agent so they make more profit

It's my job

● Set the scene for this section, and the listening, by asking students what they know about Burma. You can recycle some 'describing a destination' language from Unit 2. Use the photo and the map to help.

● Allow students to read the article and check the information they discussed.

✚ Additional activity

(all levels)
Students prepare an email to Begoña (imagining that she is a friend) asking for details of the tour for a client (see model in Writing bank 5).

Listening
The 'Peace in Burma' tour

● Allow plenty of time for **1**, to set the scene and pre-teach any vocabulary.

● 🎧 Reassure students that they do not have to pronounce the Burmese place names in **2**, just recognize them. Point out that recognizing unusual names is important in tourism.

● Pairs check answers before reporting back.

O━

2 and **3** (answers to **3** in brackets)
Places: Bagan, Inle, Mandalay, Ngapali, Thandwe, Yangon
Activities: rent a bicycle (Bagan), spend some time at the beach (Ngapali),
   visit a school of Buddhism (Mandalay), go trekking in the mountains
   (Inle), visit the city's floating markets (Inle), visit some of the many
   temples (Bagan), visit the capital city (Yangon)
4 they don't know anything about it, they're scared

Top margin

- Ask students if they think the figure would be different for their country. Do people from their country like to take package or independent holidays?

Language spot
Asking questions

- Before looking at **1**, ask students what questions they think a travel agent would want to ask tour operators at a trade fair.

- Ensure accuracy in the question forms (e.g. use of auxiliaries), but also fluency of pronunciation.

O━

2 Does the price include meals?
   Do you use local hotels?
   Do you accept groups?
   Is there a discount for groups?
   How much is the discount?
   How much is the travel agent's commission?
3 Possible answers
   Does the price include transport?
   Is there a minimum size for groups?
   Do group leaders get free travel and accommodation?
   Do you have reps at the destination?
   What services do you offer at the destination?

➕ Additional activity
(stronger students)
For **3**, ask students to write the questions in note form as in **1**. Their partners then have to create the full question.

➕ Additional activity
(all levels)
Make a sentence using as many of the words as you can from the box. Say the sentence to your partner. Pay attention to the stress in your words.

A variation of this is for the student to say the sentence, but when they come to one of the target words they hum the stress pattern only. Student B has to identify the word, thus testing stress and vocabulary together.

Pronunciation

- 🎧 Remind students of the idea of stressed syllables. Do **1** and **2** and check the answers in open class.

- After checking the answers to **3** and **4**, ask students to look at the two-syllable words in columns 1 and 2. Point out that:
  – with most nouns and adjectives, the first syllable is stressed
  – with most verbs, the second syllable is stressed.

O━

1 1st = agent, local, travel; 2nd = accept
3 •• = brochure, discount, package, transfers
   • • = include
   • • • = customer, holiday
   • • • = commission, component, domestic, inclusive, providers

Speaking

Talking to tour operators

- Set the classroom up to replicate a stall at a trade fair. If you have any brochures from India or Mexico, then use them as well.

Reading

An inclusive tour

- Write *Lithuania, Latvia, Estonia, Riga, Tallinn, Vilnius* in random order on the board. Ask students to identify which are countries and which are cities – and if possible to match them. Check by referring to the map in the book.

- Ask if they know anything more about the places.

- Do **1** in pairs. Students do **2** on their own, and then compare with a partner.

- **3** is a role-play. If you want to make the role-play a little different, give the 'clients' the role of someone famous or someone they know.

1

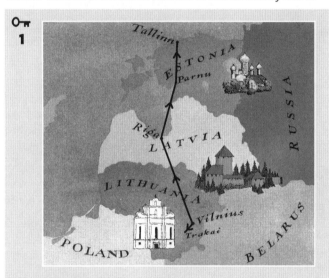

2 1 six days
2 20/7, 27/7, 3/8, 10/8
3 first-class hotels
4 $845 (based on double)
5 $1190
6 a no (just breakfast), b no, c no (arrival only)
7 yes

✚ Additional activity

(all levels)
Get students to work in pairs. A calls out a time expression (from the table or another) and B gives the preposition. Points are scored accordingly. The activity can be adapted to 'preposition tennis' – A keeps 'serving' time expressions until B gets one wrong, at which point A scores the point ('fifteen-love', etc.).

Language spot

Prepositions of time

- Do **1** and **2** in pairs, then check answers in open class.

1 at = Easter, the weekend, night, 4 o'clock
for = Easter, the weekend, the afternoon, six days, the summer, a long time
in = the afternoon, the summer, 2007
on = Sunday, 10 June
2 1 at   2 in   3 at   4 For   5 at

Customer care

The personal touch

- Give an example of an occasion when you received special personal service (invent if necessary) – e.g. someone at an airport who helped you when you were in a hurry / feeling nervous.

- Get students in pairs to do **1** and **2**, and then report back to the class.

- Some examples for tour operators might be: *a checklist of things to take / do before departure, a 24-hour helpline when you are on holiday, a personal phone call a week or two after to see if everything was fine.*

Speaking

Designing a package tour

- Explain the instructions and language exponents in **1** and **2** and then divide the class into groups. Make sure that one person is the secretary and that the group are discussing all the points in **1** (in English!).

- Gather any significant errors that you hear for later correction work, but do not interrupt the flow of the discussions.

- There are two ways of reporting back at the end: (a) The secretary of each group can give a simple presentation to the rest of the class. (b) New groups could be formed with one person from each of the original groups, and in these new groups each person can describe the tour they have planned. Other group members can ask questions and make suggestions.

✚ Additional activity

(stronger students)
If your students prefer, they can use information of their own to write their web page. Alternatively they can go to the Internet and find a tour in their own language. They print this out and then write their English version of the text.

✱ Tip

Using search engines

By now students should have accessed a number of useful websites for this sort of information (see *Find out* in Units 1 and 2). You can also show them how to use search engines such as Google to gather Tourism / ESP information. In this activity a simple Google search on 'tour operators' plus the name of their region or country should give the necessary sources.

Writing

A web page for a package tour

- Spend some time in class preparing the language for this (as well as the design of the web page). Allow enough time for students to begin the writing in class, even if you set the main writing for homework.

- Display the finished web pages in the class.

Find out

- Get students to prepare for this by researching on their own. The classroom stage will be largely a question of reporting back and correlating the information.

Writing

Describing local tour operations

- This activity follows on directly from *Find out*, and introduces another genre of tourism writing – factual reports.

Checklist, Key words, Next stop

See suggestions on p.5. Remind students about transferring vocabulary into their Personal Learning Dictionaries.

4 Tourist motivations

Background

Most tourist *arrivals statistics* classify visitors as

- Leisure tourism
- Visiting Friends and Relatives (abbreviated to VFR)
- Business tourism.

This classification reflects the *reason* for travelling.

Leisure tourism covers any activity we undertake in our free time and which produces pleasure. This includes health tourism, sports tourism (both watching and participating), educational travel, cultural and historical travel, travel for religious reasons, and so on.

There is a leisure element to *VFR*, especially in social occasions like weddings or birthdays. However, VFR is often not dependent on tourism services like accommodation. Because of this, many tourism authorities see VFR as sufficiently different from leisure tourism to be seen as a class on its own.

Business tourism covers a wide range of activities: exhibitions and fairs, conferences, business meetings, and incentive travel. People travelling on business need to relax, and they may take advantage of a business trip to visit a local tourist attraction. However, business travel is different from leisure tourism and VFR in that the main reason for travelling is work, not pleasure.

The *motivations* that cause people to travel vary enormously. It is generally felt, however, that in addition to the internal drives we all experience and that 'push' us to travel, there are other influences. The attractions at the different destinations or the popularity of a destination among our acquaintances are often said to 'pull' us into travelling.

Tourist behaviour is the way people act when they travel to other places. Sadly, not all tourist behaviour is appropriate. Of course, we often behave differently on holiday, but when that behaviour is deemed unacceptable by the culture we are visiting, problems arise. These are sometimes referred to as *culture clash*.

Travel agents and tour operators can help reduce culture clash by informing clients about behaviour at their destination. It can also be avoided if the host authorities make information available through websites, hotels, or specific tourist attractions. Well handled, it is the very nature of *cultural difference* that makes travel to exotic places interesting.

Take off

- Encourage students to think about the *reasons* for the various trips in **1**.
- Get the students to report back on some of the trips they listed in **2** and write them on the board – in particular any that are described in the reading that follows (e.g. *package holiday, cruise*). This will help with pre-teaching vocabulary for the reading. You do not need to provide any 'answers' to **3**.

1 a7 b6 c5 d4 e2

Possible answers

I love skiing. I like the fresh air and being out in the mountains – and the après-ski as well. (1)

I think it's important to study languages in the country where they are spoken, and to learn about the culture at the same time (3)

Reading

Why do people travel?

- Focus students on the task – in **1**, looking for the things they listed and categorizing them.

- Draw a circle with three segments on the board and get the students to write (or shout out) the types of holiday for each segment.

∗ Tip

Pie charts

In **3** these can either be done as individual, small group, or whole class projects. The charts can either be hand-drawn or use an Excel application. Display the results.

Listening

Reasons for travel and money spent on travel

- Do some revision of number pronunciation before they listen.

- 🎧 Play the listening twice, with pairs checking their answers each time.

---

1 a Leisure 53%, VFR 32%, Business 11%, Other 4%
 b Leisure 70%, Business 16%, VFR 11%, Other 3%
2 Possible answer
 With VFR, tourists often stay with their family or friends (so there are no accommodation costs) and do not visit so many sights.

✚ Additional activity

(stronger students)

Mask the words in column A to see if students can identify the definition (some of the words have occurred before).

Vocabulary

Reasons for travel

- Do the first two in **1** in open class. Get students to work in pairs for the others. **2** can be done in open class, and then work in pairs for **3**.

---

1 and **2**

1 c – Leisure	5 f – Business	9 e – Leisure
2 g – Business	6 l – VFR	10 d – Leisure
3 i – Leisure	7 k – Leisure	11 h – Business
4 a – Leisure	8 b – Leisure	12 j – Business

Listening

Passenger survey

- Use **1** to familiarize students with the pronunciation of the place names they will hear in the listening.

- 🎧 After the first listening, report back on **2**, and ask students if they can fill in any of the information for the table in **3**. Then listen again. The students can complete the sentences in **4** and then check with the listening script.

3

	Where from?	Destination	Purpose	Length of stay
1	Pakistan	Mecca	pilgrimage	a week or so
2	Italy	Bangkok	fam trip	5 days
3	London	New York	wedding	4 days (maybe more)
4	Argentina	London	study tour	4 weeks

4 1 to help   3 because we want   5 for a business
   2 to visit   4 in case

Top margin

- Ask students what they think are the three biggest religions in the world (1 Christianity: 2.1 billion, 2 Islam: 1.3 billion, 3 Hinduism: 900 million), and to guess how many Muslims there are in the world today. Do they know any holy sites for Muslims?

Language spot
Talking about reason

- Do an example match in class first. Students work in pairs and report back after each activity.

1 1 c 2 f 3 h 4 e 5 a 6 g 7 b 8 d
2 3, 4, 6, and 8
3 1 to   3 because   5 because, because of
   2 in case   4 for
4 2 (in case)
5 1 to   3 in case   5 for, to
   2 because of   4 because

Pronunciation

- Play or read the three countries in **1**. Invite your students to describe the differences in their own words. Ask them to say each word in **2** in pairs, thinking about these differences.

- Play the recording for **3**. Repeat if necessary, then check the answers.

- Ask students to look at the spelling of the /dʒ/ sound. Bring out the 'ge' spelling for this sound. Tell them that the spelling 'gi' (e.g. *religious*) also often makes this sound. Repeat this process for the sound /tʃ/ and the spelling 'ch'.

Where in the world?

- Brainstorm what students know about Kenya. Lead them to speculate on the type of holidays in Kenya as well as facts on population, capital, and climate.

- Students will confirm by listening to the interview and reading the article and the factoid.

Listening
Interview with a Kenyan tour operator

- Get students to read through the questions first, so that they are familiar with the vocabulary.

- Play the listening twice, with pairs comparing answers in between listenings. **2** sets the scene for *Reading*.

1 1 39, 1994, 2000   3 25%
   2 meeting diverse people   4 beach, swimming, safari, hiking, culture, golf, camel rides

✱ Tip
in case
Students may have problems with *in case* as it functions differently to the other purpose conjunctions, and refers to a reason that might happen. **4** brings direct attention to this.

✱ Tip
Monolingual classes
If you are working with a monolingual group, point out to the class which of these sounds exist in their mother tongue, and concentrate on the others.

✚ Additional activity
(all levels)
Get the students to use the map of Kenya and the information in the interview with John Muhoho to plan an itinerary for a tour of Kenya, revising the work of Unit 3.

Top margin

- Ask general questions, before they read the fact: *Where in Africa do tourists go? Is tourism growing in Africa? What do tourists look for in Africa?*

Reading

The changing face of tourism

- Help students to think about changes in tourism in the last twenty or thirty years by asking them about holidays their parents had when they were young.

- Question 3 in **1** provides an opportunity to pre-teach vocabulary.

- Get students to discuss their answers in pairs after reading, and give the class time to discuss the answers to **3**.

1 3 'old' = high-rise, concrete, package
'new' = authentic, independent, fly-drive, long-haul, ecotourism

3 Possible answers

In Africa	Old tourism	New tourism
1	See lions; lie by the pool	Horse riding; hillwalking
2	Food from own country	Traditional food with local people
3	Large concrete hotels	Simple tents and lodges
4	International tour operators	Local Xhosa guides

In general	Old tourism	New tourism
1	Sun and sea package holiday	Independent, fly-drive, tailor-made
2	Two weeks	Shorter
3	—	Adventure, cultural, sports, ecotourism
4	—	Faraway places: China, Maldives, Botswana, Vanuatu

Language spot

Describing trends

- Establish the time frame by drawing a time line on the board. Use the time line to indicate tense use: Past Simple, Present Perfect, Present Continuous.

- Get students to do the activities in pairs and report back to the whole class.

1 and **2**
1 b, e, f (Present Continuous)
2 a, c (Past Simple)
3 d (Present Perfect)
3
Instead they **are looking for** more authentic experiences.
More and more tourists **are looking for** adventure, activity, and authenticity.
Adventure travel, ecotourism, cultural tours, and sports vacations **are taking** people to more exotic destinations.

4 up = rise, increase, grow; down = decrease, fall, drop
5 gradually – steadily – sharply – dramatically
6 **Possible answers**
2 The number of people taking weekend city breaks is rising sharply.
3 The number of people going on long-haul flights is increasing gradually.
4 The number of people choosing beach holidays is falling sharply.
5 The number of people making online holiday bookings is growing dramatically.
6 The number of (people using) High Street travel agents is dropping dramatically.

Find out

- Set the scene by talking through the questions and discussing ideas and approaches. For example, for **2**, students can interview their parents and older members of their family.

- Students research the questions and bring back the raw data for further class discussion and *Writing*.

Writing
Your country or region

- This can be done as homework or as a longer course assignment. Encourage students to use a variety of ways of displaying the information – pie charts, tables (e.g. like the one on p.33 of the Student's Book).

- Students should show each other the finished results – and display them on the classroom wall.

Speaking
Changes in tourist motivation

- Give students time to read their information files and relate them to **1**. Explain any vocabulary – e.g. *switch off*.

- In **3**, make sure students are using the language of describing trends.

Customer care
'We know what you want ...'

- Ask students for their experience of being asked what they want (e.g. being stopped in the street, or being phoned up). Use their experiences (or your own if they don't have any) to establish the importance of balancing helping tourists to fulfil their dreams and not being too intrusive.

Checklist, Key words, Next stop

- See suggestions on p.5. Remind students about transferring vocabulary into their Personal Learning Dictionaries.

✱ Tip
Course portfolio
As well as using assignments like this as displays in the class, students can build up a personal portfolio (which may be useful when applying for jobs, work experience, or further training).

➕ Additional activity
(stronger students)
Get students to write a report on general trends in tourist motivations, using the information from the *Speaking* activity and also from the 'Old and new tourism' article.

➕ Additional activity
(all levels)
Role-play some survey situations, with people being stopped in the street. Give some of the interviewees 'attitude' cards, such as *in a hurry, cooperative, angry, talkative*.

5 Travel agencies

Background

Travel agents are *retailers*; they sell tourism products to the public in a shop that is called a *travel agency*. They are part of the *chain of distribution* and connect tour operators (the *wholesalers*) to customers.

Travel agencies sell a range of products and services:

Products can be thought of as items created by other companies which the travel agent sells for commission. Typical products are

- package holidays
- air, train, and coach tickets
- traveller's cheques
- insurance.

Services involve

- guiding and advising customers as to the best product
- giving advice on visa and passport applications
- planning travel itineraries and working out costs
- representing a client in a complaint procedure after an unsatisfactory holiday.

The amount of *commission* varies, being as low as 1% for traveller's cheques, and as high as 40% for travel insurance. Commission on package holidays is often around 10%, while commission on air tickets is now lower than it used to be as major airlines turn to the Internet for their ticket sales. To counter this, travel agents are increasingly charging a set *fee* for issuing air, train, or coach tickets, obtaining visas, or booking a hotel room.

Most tourism students will work as a travel agency sales consultant when they first begin to work in this sector. This is a demanding job, and one requiring a wide range of different *skills* and *qualities*, such as

- a very wide knowledge of geography
- detailed knowledge of the products the agency offers
- high-level computer skills, especially for
  - using the Internet to research destinations
  - using computer reservation systems to put together airfares or make other bookings
- excellent personal skills, especially good listening skills
- the ability to determine a client's needs accurately.

Travel agency sales follow a clearly structured procedure known as the *sales process*. Some sources show this with as few as four *stages*, others as many as eight, but all models of sales contain four main stages:

- establishing rapport with the client
- investigating the client's needs
- presenting the product
- getting the client to commit themselves to the purchase.

Ownership of travel agencies varies considerably. A significant proportion of travel agencies are actually part of a large company with a chain of agencies distributed around the major cities in a country. In addition, many tour operators have their own travel agencies to promote and sell their products.

Take off

- Ask students about local travel agencies. Are they similar to the ones in the pictures? Students discuss the questions in pairs then report back to the class.

Listening
All in a day's work

- In **1**, discuss the ten products and services in pairs or open class. Make sure students are familiar with all the terms. Ask some check questions, e.g. *Which one will help a tourist get permission to enter a country? Which one will help a tourist to get money if something bad happens?*

- Ask if the students have ever bought any of the products or services.

- 🎧 In **2**, pause the recording after each customer to give time to write the answers. Students check answers in pairs and then report back.

○━

1 Free = 1, 3, 9. The others usually make a profit for the travel agency.
2 1 airline tickets   4 foreign currency / advice on visas
   2 hotel bookings   5 travel insurance
   3 package holidays

Reading

The sales process

● Warm up to this by asking students if they have ever been 'sold' a service or product. A good way to elicit this is to ask them what was the biggest item they've ever bought. Try to identify any stages or tactics that the salesperson used.

● Focus attention on the flow diagram. Explain any difficult vocabulary (e.g. *raising awareness, rapport*). Get students to read through the six questions before they read the text. Compare answers in pairs before reporting back.

○━

Possible answers
1 Stage 4
2 Stage 3
3 Adverts in the local press, on local radio and TV, leaflets and flyers left in bars and supermarkets, etc.
4 If you talk to them, they will feel under pressure, think that you are trying to force them to buy, and will probably leave the agency.
5 Benefits – these can only be explained with respect to the needs and preferences of the individual client.
6 Closing the sale is done when the customer returns to the agency to book their holiday. After-sales service is given when the customer has returned from holiday.

➕ Additional activity

(stronger students)
Get students to make their own gap-fill exercise by writing a sentence similar to the ones in the text.

✳ Tip

PLD reminder
Remind students about the Personal Learning Dictionary – not just for this vocabulary activity, but for the reading before it as well. At this stage in the course, it might be useful to ask students to hand in their PLDs as a way of checking their work in this area.

➕ Additional activity

(weaker students)
Allow students to read through the dialogue first.
Pause the listening at appropriate moments during the second listening.

Vocabulary

Sales terms

● Get students to find the words in the text and try to work out their meaning from the context, before doing the matching activity. Check answers in pairs. Report back after each activity. Students will need dictionaries for **4**.

○━

1 and **2**
1 consultant – noun   4 advantage – noun
2 benefit – noun (but can also be a verb)   5 browse – verb
3 awareness – noun   6 convince – verb
3 1 consultant   3 advantage   5 browse
   2 awareness   4 benefit

Listening

A new customer

● Use the pictures to set the scene.

- 🎧 In **1**, make sure students concentrate on what the travel agent says. In **2**, they will need to listen to both the travel agent and the customer.

> 🔑
> **1** 1 stages 2 and 3 (establishing rapport and investigating needs)
>   2 yes
> **2** 1 T 2 F 3 F 4 T 5 F 6 F
> **3** **Possible answer** Yes, she makes the customers feel relaxed and finds out what they want and need. She is on course to make a sale.

✳ Tip
'Open' v 'closed' questions
In tourism sales situations like this, it is often preferable to ask open questions, which allow the sales consultant to find out more about the customer and adjust their product selection and presentation accordingly.

Language spot
'Open' and 'closed' questions

- 🎧 Students can predict or try to remember the gap-fills before listening.

- Report back on **1** and answer **2**, **3**, and **4** in open class. Get students to work in pairs on **5**.

> 🔑
> **1** 1 help   3 your, way
>   2 thinking, package tour   4 exactly, travel
> **2** 1 and 2
> **3** 3 – with a place name (in Melbourne)
>   4 – with a date (ideally on the 20th of July).
> **4** closed questions can only be answered with *yes, no,* or *I don't know*; open questions usually require fuller answers
> **5** **Possible answers**
>   1 How long do you want to be in Australia?
>   2 Which places do you want to visit?
>   3 Where do you want to stay?
>   4 How many of you are travelling?
>   5 What time of year do you want to go?
>   6 How much do you want to spend?
>   7 How often do you go there?

Top margin

- For students with more knowledge and experience of working in tourism, you can discuss the different levels of commission for different products, and how they have changed, and are likely to change.

Speaking
Investigating a client's needs

- Before starting the role-play, get students to practise making the questions from the prompts on the sales enquiry form.

- Divide the class into groups of three and set up chairs to simulate a travel agency. Make it clear that there will be three separate role-plays, with each student getting a chance to be a sales consultant to two customers.

- Monitor the role-plays, noting any errors. Do not intervene unless communication breaks down. At the end, discuss with the whole class how they felt, what they found difficult, and if they felt they improved.

➕ Additional activity
(weaker students)
Get students to read through and act out the script of the listening on page 38 before they start the freer activity here.

➕ Additional activity
(stronger students)
Use a drama technique for the role-play. This will test the sales consultant's ability to determine needs. Get the 'customer' to think of a need (e.g. a particular type of holiday they want to enquire about). The customer can't speak and can only use mime or facial reactions to communicate and 'answer' the sales consultant's questions.

Customer care

Identifying needs

- Use the cartoon to discuss ways of determining a customer's needs. Are they in a hurry? Do they look unsure or decided? Is there any way of identifying someone who is going to be a waste of time?

It's my job

- Ask students to look at the pictures and think of a question that they would like to ask Michaela, then read through to see if it is answered.

- After they have read the interview, get students to discuss the stage of the sales process that they think Michaela is good at. The most probable answer is Stage 2, but they might be able to justify other answers.

Find out

- Some students may find this challenging as they are being asked to take on an investigative role. However, this is balanced by the fact that they will probably be working in their own language (but reporting back in English).

Writing

A report on a travel agency

- Students can write their reports for homework.

- Get students to explain their reports to a partner. The partner should ask questions about the details. Display the reports on the wall or in a class folder.

Listening

Presenting a product

- 🎧 This is a continuation of the conversation on page **38** and students will already know a little about the customers and their needs. Students can therefore speculate before they listen. This will familiarize them with the contents of the tours and the questions.

- Students should compare answers in pairs after each listening task and report back to class.

> **1** 1 Ayers Rock
> 2 Great Barrier Reef
> 3 All Australia and Australia's Best
> **2** 1 19 days, 13 days
> 2 train, plane, coach
> 3 hotel, full-board or half-board
> **3** 1 should, my opinion
> 2 you, I'd take
> 3 think about

✱ Tip

Reviews of tourism provision

This is the first activity in the book where students are asked to review a tourism service provider. It is an extremely useful and authentic way of putting the theory of the unit content into practice. It can be repeated later with other tourism service providers (hotels, airports, etc.).

✚ Additional activity

(all levels)

Prepare an email confirming Karl and Anita's booking (see Writing bank 3 for a model).

Language spot
Suggestions and advice

● Get students to do **1** and **2** in pairs.

● Get students to think of the tourist statement that might come before the suggestion or advice. This will help with the mini-dialogue work in **3**.

> **1** 1 d   2 e/f   3 e/f   4 a   5 c   6 b
> **2** 1 a/c   2 a/c   3 e   4 d   5 f   6 b

Pronunciation

● Check students can pronounce the letters at the top of the columns. Sometimes linking them to a lexical set can help, e.g. colours – *grey, green, red, white, rose, blue, dark*. Pause the recording if necessary.

Speaking
Suggesting alternatives and making a recommendation

● Give students time to read their roles. In **1**, the role-play should concentrate on the advice and suggestion language.

● **2** could be a lengthy role-play and it is important to allow plenty of time. They will be bringing together all the language from the unit. Help the role-play develop by writing the six stages of the sales process on the board as a reminder.

Reading
The impact of the Internet

● This may be challenging for some students, so set it up carefully. Divide the board in two – one half headed *Travel Agents*, the other *Internet*. Ask students to think about the advantages of each for buying / selling travel products.

● Refer the students to the 'five popular myths' in **1**. Do they agree with them? Think of arguments *against* the myths. Read to find out which of the myths are discussed and check answers.

> **1** Myth 1 is not discussed.
> **3** Reality: Every travel agency is different and accordingly, some are better suited to a given consumer than others.

Checklist, Key words, Next stop

● See suggestions on p.5. Remind students about transferring vocabulary into their Personal Learning Dictionaries.

See suggestions on p.5.

∗ Tip
Spelling out

When you work in an international industry like tourism you meet names of places and people that are completely new to you, or are being given in different languages. Because of this it is very important to be able to understand and produce accurate spelling – sometimes face-to-face, sometimes on the phone.

∗ Tip
Recording students

Being recorded can be daunting at first for students, but in an industry like tourism, where oral production and oral / aural skills in general are so important, it is an extremely effective learning and teaching strategy. Be sensitive in the early stages – for example, always try to balance correction with praise.

➕ Additional activity
(all levels)

After you have marked and returned the recording, get the students to re-record the same conversation. Hopefully, this time they will avoid some of the errors you have corrected and repeat and expand areas you have praised.

6 Transport in tourism

Background

Transport is one of the six sub-sectors of the tourism industry. It is usually divided into

- *surface* (land) *transport* – train, coach, bus, tram, taxi, car, motorbike, and bicycle
- *water-borne transport* – cruise ship (liner), ferry, hydrofoil, hovercraft, yacht, motorboat, and barge
- *air transport* – jet aircraft, light aircraft, and helicopter.

From the tourist's point of view, each of these modes fulfils one of three functions:

- travel to and from the destination
- local transport at the destination
- transport as a tourist attraction.

Air transport is the dominant form of travel to and from today's tourist destinations. Units 9 and 12 look at air transport in depth.

Trains provide transport to and from destinations and also locally. They can also be a tourist attraction, as with the Orient Express from Paris to Venice. *Coaches* provide international and inter-city transport. In those countries where the rail network is not well developed, *luxury coaches* provide a cheap but comfortable alternative. This is the case in much of South America.

Buses, *trams*, and *taxis* offer *urban* transport once at the destination, whilst the private car, or a *hire car*, offers local and inter-city transport. *Helicopters* are increasingly used as air taxis in big cities, but they can also be an attraction

in their own right. The motorbike and bicycle provide local transport for a minority of tourists in some destinations.

Modern *cruise ships* are floating hotels, and provide transport, accommodation, and attractions in a single place. Not all cruises take place at sea. The Nile in Egypt and the Rhine in Germany are rivers where tourists can enjoy cruises. Cruise ships are normally supported by some form of land transport for local travel at each stopping point.

Ferries travel between countries, as with the cross-channel ferries from the UK to continental Europe, or between islands, as in Greece or the Philippines. *Hydrofoils* travel at high speed above the surface of the water supported on skis, and *hovercraft* travel on water and land by 'floating' on a cushion of air.

Tourism transport can be *scheduled* or *charter*:

- *Scheduled* transport operates on a regular basis shown on a published *timetable* and following specific routes. Scheduled transport is obliged to travel even if there are no passengers, which can make it expensive.
- *Charter* transport is aircraft, coaches, or trains that have been contracted (usually by a tour operator) to travel to a specific destination on a specific date. The plane / coach / train will normally travel full, and so charter transport is cheaper than scheduled.

Shuttle services are air or land connections between two points that leave as soon as the plane, coach, or bus is full, and do not follow a strict timetable. Most major hotels have shuttle buses to pick up guests from the local airport.

Take off

- Discuss the questions in small groups and report back to the whole class. Ensure correct pronunciation of country names. To check answers, students work in groups. Each group is assigned a route and looks up their route in an atlas or on a world map.
- Use **2** to find out what transport vocabulary they already know. Write the transport in three columns on the board: *air*, *water*, and *land*.

✳ Tip

Vocabulary revision

There is lots of vocabulary in this unit, so use it as an opportunity to revise the PLD, word groups, charts and grids, and collocation.

Vocabulary

Transport words

- Check answers to the gap-fill and subsequent activities in pairs. Students look back at previous units to find words to add (for **2**).

✳ Tip

American English v British English
Draw attention to the differences between BrE and AmE (e.g. *motorway / freeway*, *petrol station / gas station*) – especially as a lot of the material in this unit is American-based. Get students to start a separate page in their notes on BrE v AmE – and note that it won't just be lexical differences, but things like the 24-hour clock, the layout conventions for timetables, etc.

➕ Additional activity

(stronger students)
Plan a route round the world which uses at least twelve different types of transport. Write up the itinerary (as in Unit 3).

➕ Additional activity

(all levels)
Look back at the word lists for Units 1 to 5. Find two more words for each of the columns. Make an alphabetical list of the words, and ask your partner to pronounce them and put them in the right column.

➕ Additional activity

(stronger students)
Invite students to look for sound–spelling relationships for the words in each column. For example, the words with the diphthong /aɪ/ all have the spelling 'i'+consonant+final 'e'.

1

1	land	8	cruises	15	train
2	long-haul	9	cabins	16	terminus
3	flight	10	stewards	17	stations
4	airports	11	purser	18	carriages
5	terminal	12	crossings	19	coaches
6	runway	13	port	20	motorways
7	helicopter	14	harbour	21	tour guide

3

Method of travel	Transport types	Places and features	Tourism professionals
Air	shuttle		
Water	yacht	marina	captain
Land	taxi hire car jeep shuttle	freeway service station scenic route tunnel	ticket collector

Find out

- Students will need to visit the sources of data they identified in Unit 1 – and add the names and websites of national carriers and transport organizations. The prediction stage should be done in class and will involve students in free practice of some transport vocabulary.

Top margin

- Students can compare the data about their own countries in *Find out* with the information on the USA. Ask if any of the information surprises them.

Pronunciation

- 🎧 Get students to do **1** in pairs. Check the answers in open class.
- 🎧 Play the recording again for **2**, asking the students to concentrate on the length of the vowel sounds. In **3**, ask students to make a short, chopping movement with their hands for short sounds, and a long, sweeping movement for long sounds.

1

ten /e/	see /iː/	day /eɪ/
ferry	clean	plane
jet	easy	safe
leisure	scenic	train

2 ten

4

hat /æ/	arm /ɑː/	five /aɪ/
track	car	drive
	craft	guide
	fast	ride
	guard	
	harbour	

Vocabulary
Adjectives describing transport

- Students work in pairs in **1**. They should also mark the stress on the words with two or more syllables. Report back by getting one pair to shout out one of their adjectives, and another pair to shout out its opposite. Correct pronunciation if necessary. In **2**, make sure they use positive adjectives for the first two gaps and a negative one for the last.

> ⚷
> **1** boring – exciting   crowded – quiet
> cheap – expensive   dangerous – safe
> clean – dirty   difficult – easy
> comfortable – uncomfortable   fast – slow
>   punctual – unpunctual

Language spot
Comparing things

- Set the situation of a journey to another city. Write the words *train* and *coach* on different halves of the board, and elicit arguments in favour of each, using the adjectives from *Vocabulary*. Write one or two of the comparative sentences on the board (but not the ones in the activity).

- Students do the activities in pairs and then report back.

> ⚷
> **1** 1 faster, fastest   2 easiest   3 more comfortable
> 4 fast   5 comfortable
> **2** See Grammar reference p.122.

Speaking
What is most important for tourists when travelling?

- In whole class, brainstorm what things are important for the students when they travel – speed, comfort, punctuality, and so on.

- Put students in groups of three or four and look at the four transport situations in **1**. Get them to think of other important criteria, for example: *At the airport – somewhere to lie down and sleep, a quiet area, a games area; On a train – quiet carriages with no mobile phones, good food and drink.*

- Make sure they come up with a clear order in **2**. They should appoint one spokesperson to present their opinions to the class.

Customer care
Exceeding expectations

- Encourage students to think of basic ideas first – e.g. *free drinks, magazines, a route map.* They can then think of more exotic ideas – e.g. *use of binoculars on a coach, personal stereos, guided audio tours, someone to carry their bags for them.*

- If they have problems thinking of things, you can give them a list like this and ask them to rank them. Lead into a discussion on first-class travel – how it is different, why people choose it, etc.

Listening
Transport systems and cable cars in San Francisco

- 🎧 Get students to read through the list of transport types. They can predict the answers to the questions before listening, if you want.

- Pairs check answers. Play the listening again if necessary.

> 🔑
> 1 ferries, buses, metro, trains, cable cars, bike rental, coach tours, car hire
> 2 1873, three, 6 a.m. to 1 a.m., Monday through Sunday, $3, any stop with a brown cable-car sign

✳ Tip
Authentic timetables
Bring in other authentic timetables for different transport types in the town or city where you are studying (there may be English language versions). Compare the different style and layout of the timetables with the San Francisco ones. Use them for short role-plays.

Additional activity
(all levels)
Students prepare a fax cover sheet for a client, with one of the timetables from p.48 (see Writing bank 6 for a model).

Reading
San Francisco transport timetables and schedules

- Divide the class into groups of three. Each student focuses on a different timetable, A, B, or C. When they have looked at the timetables, the students should get together and answer the questions. These are really just scanning questions – the timetables are going to be used for further exploitation in the *Language spot* and *Speaking* that follow.

> 🔑
> **1** 1 a   6 c
> 2 b, c   7 b (outside rush hours), c
> 3 a (Muir Woods), c   8 a, b (during rush hours)
> 4 a (Alcatraz)   9 a (Muir Woods)
> 5 b   10 a – service dogs only
> **2** 1 d   2 c   3 e   4 a   5 b

Language spot
Describing a timetable

- Ask students to produce a similar sentence for each of the four language areas to show they understand the grammatical features.

- Students do **1** and **2** on their own and then compare answers in pairs before reporting back to the whole class.

> 🔑
> **1** The cable cars **run from** 6 a.m. **to** 1 a.m. Monday through Sunday.
> At peak times they **are** approximately every five **to** ten minutes.
> Tickets **can** be bought at special booths.
> You **can** board at any of the stops indicated with the brown cable-car sign.
> Cable-car riders **should** hold on tight.
> **2**
> 1 depart/leave   5 at   9 at
> 2 every   6 at   10 4.30
> 3 leaves/departs   7 2.15 p.m. 11 daily
> 4 from   8 leaves   12 cannot

✚ Additional activity
(all levels)
Repeat a similar simulation using authentic local timetables, and record the dialogue for correction and praise.

Speaking
Timetable information

● Divide the class in half for **1**. It is important that they do not look at the texts, so there should be a mixture of questions answered by the texts and questions not answered by the texts.

● Ensure students are forming correct questions at this preparation stage.

● Pair the students up, one from each group, and do **2**, with the travel information officers referring to their texts (the cable-car listening script or the Amtrak schedule). Encourage the information officers to invent appropriate answers for questions they don't have information on – and to deal with all questions politely.

Writing
Transport and timetable information

● This activity brings together all the themes of the unit and can be set as a homework assignment. Try to find some examples of city transport websites to help students.

● Display finished work on the wall or in a class folder.

Where in the world?

● Allow plenty of time to look at the picture and take from it whatever they want. **1** to **4** can be answered in pairs or small groups.

✚ Additional activity
(all levels)
Ask students to decide which three places the following people would enjoy on the cruise ship.
● A newly-married couple in their 20s
● A retired couple in their 70s
● A man in his 40s recovering from a serious operation and travelling on his own
● A family group of four consisting of the two grandparents and two young children (aged four and seven)
● A woman in her 30s on her very first trip out of her own country
They can also write some passenger profiles of their own – including people they know – and pass to other students to decide.

Listening
A cruise ship worker

● Use **1** to familiarize students with the general content of the listening. Check / pre-teach key vocabulary – e.g. *waiter, interview, CV, day off, off duty, passengers*.

● 🎧 You will probably need to play the listening twice. Students can compare answers after the first listening.

2 1 junior waiter in four-star hotel (training as waiter including silver-service); deputy head waiter in French restaurant in Manchester
2 CV and photo
3 Miami
4 long hours of work, no regular weekly day off, not allowed to go ashore, not allowed to mix with the passengers or use passenger facilities
5 own social facilities, food and accommodation are free, amazing social life

Checklist, Key words, Next stop

● See suggestions on p.5. Remind students about transferring vocabulary into their Personal Learning Dictionaries.

7 Accommodation

Background

Tourist accommodation is one of the six sub-sectors of the tourism industry. It can be classified as:

Serviced accommodation. This refers to any sort of accommodation where the guests receive a place to sleep, meals, porter services, reception services, and so on. Typical examples of serviced accommodation are

- hotels
- motels
- guest houses
- bed and breakfast.

Self-catering accommodation. In this sort of accommodation the guests prepare their own meals, and very few other services are provided except for reception. Types of self-catering accommodation include

- apartments
- campsites
- caravans
- motorhomes
- villas.

Hotels are the most popular type of accommodation in many countries. They can be small, family-owned hotels, hotels at popular resorts catering for holidaymakers, business hotels, and so on.

All hotels offer a range of *services* and *facilities*.
- *Services* involve a member of the hotel staff doing something for you. Typical services are reception services, transportation and transfers, tourist information, ticket reservations, laundry, and room service.
- *Facilities* make the guest's stay more enjoyable, and include restaurants and bars, business centres, sports facilities, minibar, pay TV, internet connection in room, direct dial telephone, and so on.

Depending on the range of services and facilities on offer, a hotel can be classified as 1-star through to 5-star. The star rating system is the *classification* that is used most around the world. Other systems exist, but all of them essentially classify hotels as luxury, superior, mid-market, and budget / economy.

Reservations for hotels can be taken in different ways:
- face-to-face in the hotel
- by phone
- by email, fax, or in writing using a conventional letter
- through a travel agent
- through the Internet.

Internet bookings are increasingly common and use computer reservation systems like Sabre or Apollo. Major hotel chains usually have their own system. Hotel receptionists are trained to follow strict procedures when entering information about a reservation into the hotel reservation system.

✚ Additional activity

(all levels)
Devise a *Find someone who*, by giving each student something different to find out about the other class members, for example:
Find someone who
- likes camping
- knows someone who works in a hotel
- stayed in a hotel last year
- can name three different types of accommodation
- has stayed in a five-star hotel
- would like to work on a cruise ship
etc.

✳ Tip

Venn diagrams

Venn diagrams are another useful visual way of storing vocabulary. Look back at other units to find vocabulary where it could be useful – e.g. jobs in different types of transport.

Take off

- Get students to discuss **1** to **3** in pairs or small groups and then report back.

Vocabulary

Types of accommodation

- Discuss **1** and **2** in open class. Work through **3** and **4** in pairs and report back.

○┳
1, 3 and **4 Possible answers**

	3	4.1	4.2
apartment	self-catering	both	static
bed and breakfast	serviced	both	static
campsite (picture 4)	self-catering	both	static
caravan (picture 1)	self-catering	both	mobile
chalet	self-catering	both	static
country house	serviced	rural	static
cruise ship	serviced	neither	mobile

	3	4.1	4.2
farmhouse (picture 6)	both	rural	static
guest house	serviced	both	static
hostel	both	both	static
hotel (picture 5)	serviced	both	static
lodge	serviced	rural	static
log cabin (picture 2)	self-catering	rural	static
motel (picture 3)	both	both	static
motorhome	self-catering	both	mobile
mountain refuge	both	rural	static
university hall of residence	both	urban	static
villa	self-catering	both	static

Find out

- In class, discuss the types of accommodation that would suit the profiles. Students then research outside class time and report back.

- The material from this activity will feed into *Writing* on p.65.

* Tip

Hotel descriptions

Encourage students to bring in descriptions of hotels – from their local area, or where they have stayed in the past. These can be used for general reference or for role-plays later on.

Reading

What makes a good hotel?

- When the pairs have made their lists in **1**, pool all the ideas on the board and find out the most popular. Use the photos to generate interest and pre-teach any vocabulary you feel may be useful (but remember this is primarily a skimming exercise).

> **2 Possible answers**
> 1 Radisson   2 Radisson

Top margin

- Discuss if students think the trend in hotel capacity will continue, and what changes there have been in hotel accommodation in their country.

➕ Additional activity

(all levels)
Invite students to add further services and facilities to the list and to design icons for them.

* Tip

Giving opinions

Ensure students have ready access to opinion language – giving an opinion, agreeing and disagreeing with an opinion, asking for an opinion.

Vocabulary

Services and facilities

- To find out how much students already know, get them to cover the words and try to guess the names for the icons.

- Work in pairs and report back on **1**. Check pronunciation.

- Students can work on **2** on their own, but encourage as much discussion as possible at **3**, as this will maximize practice of the vocabulary.

> | | | | | |
> |---|---|---|---|---|
> | 1 a | 6 g | 11 m | 16 o | 21 q |
> | 2 b | 7 f | 12 j | 17 u | 22 s |
> | 3 d | 8 h | 13 n | 18 p | 23 w |
> | 4 c | 9 i | 14 t | 19 v | |
> | 5 e | 10 k | 15 l | 20 r | |

Language spot
Describing location

- Find the El Hana examples in open class. Students then work on their own on the two other hotels and report back to pairs.

- Use authentic hotel descriptions for the area if you have any.

> **1** *on* a 400-acre farm
> *20 miles east* of Cork City
> *in* pleasant rural surroundings
> *5 km from* several seaside villages
> *located on* the famous Promenade des Anglais
> *between* the romantic old town *and* the Arenas Business Park
> *a five-minute drive from* Nice International Airport
> *a ten-minute walk from* the train station

Speaking
Giving information about hotels

- Make sure students understand their roles. Monitor the role-plays carefully, but avoid interrupting, unless the conversation has completely broken down or students are using their L1. Report back at the end – balancing work on errors with praise for good practice.

It's my job

- Ask students to think of three questions that they would ask a campsite owner, before they read and answer the questions in the introduction.

Listening
A place to stay

- The listening extracts are quite short and students will only hear the caller, not the tourism provider on the other end.

- Get students to predict some of the words they might hear (e.g. *double / single / twin*). This is a useful vocabulary revision activity.

- 🎧 They will probably need to listen more than once, and they can also compare answers in pairs between listenings.

Speaker	Type	Number / guests	Length of stay	Other details
Richard	hotel	1	one night	non-smoking room
Susan	hotel	2	two nights	en-suite washbasin and shower; supper
Radka	campsite	5	two weeks	from 22 July; as far as possible from the showers

➕ Additional activity
(weaker students)
Before the students pair up into A and B pairs, get groups of As and groups of Bs to read carefully through their roles together and ask each other questions to check they understand the content. This will not only help them when they come to perform the role-plays, it will also give them valuable general question-forming practice.

➕ Additional activity
(stronger students)
Prepare an email or letter enquiring about seasonal work in the campsite (see Writing bank 2 for a model).

➕ Additional activity
(all levels)
Students look at the scripts and write some of the questions that the person on the other end of the phone might have asked.

* Tip
Using websites
Whenever you use information from a website like this in class, encourage students to look up the website in their own time and explore the original, following links that interest them and so on. (This is suggested directly to the students in the *Speaking* activity on page 65.)

* Tip
Collocation as learning aid
Encourage students always to try to learn any new words with a collocation – i.e. not just *hotel*, but *five-star hotel*; not just *reservation*, but *make a reservation*.

✛ Additional activity
(all levels)
Ask students to match the adjectives to the other accommodation types in the vocabulary activity on page 60.

* Tip
Presentations
Although at this stage students will probably not need to do formal presentations, you can nevertheless make them aware of the different ways of presenting information like this – audio-visual, posters, Powerpoint. Even if they aren't using these media, they can still discuss which would be best in a 'real' presentation.

Reading
Accommodation in Scotland

- Start by asking the class if anyone has been to Scotland. What type of accommodation did they stay in? If no one has been to Scotland, get students to say what they know about Scotland, its climate, its history, etc., and then just brainstorm the types of accommodation they would expect.

- Encourage discussion when reporting back on **2**. For example: *What would it be like to stay in a lighthouse? Why are no campsites mentioned?*

> ⚷
> **2** 1 hotels, country houses, bed and breakfasts, self-catering apartments
>   2 campsites
>   3 a converted church, a former lighthouse, a medieval castle

Vocabulary
Describing accommodation: adjectives and nouns

- This activity provides further work on collocation. In **1**, ask why *metropolitan cottage* is wrong (*metropolitan* is to do with the city, *cottage* is in the countryside). Make it clear that the activity does not consist of single direct matches. Some of the matches are grey areas, but encourage students to experiment.

> ⚷
> **2** Possible answers
>   1 h, j   4 g, h   7 e   9 a, e
>   2 d, f, h, j 5 b, d, e, f, g, h, i   8 a, f, h, j   10 a, h, j
>   3 e   6 h
> **3** adjective that describes most nouns: friendly
>   adjectives that combine with only one noun: converted, metropolitan, medieval

Speaking
Unusual accommodation

- Ask students what is the most unusual place that they have stayed in. Use the pictures and the descriptions to stimulate interest in unusual accommodation. Ask them to imagine why guests would choose it.

- Help students with language functions and gambits during **4**: the discussion stage (informal), and **5**: the presentation (more formal). At the end students can vote on which of the ideas they thought was best.

Writing
Local accommodation

- This activity brings together many of the points in the unit and could be used as a major coursework assignment.

- In class get students to brainstorm ideas and approaches, not just to content and language, but to design as well.

- Present the finished articles on the wall or in a coursework portfolio.

➕ Additional activity

(weaker students)
Give students more practice of numbers and spelling by asking them to write down the name and credit card details of an imaginary person and then dictate it to their partner, asking for clarification if necessary.

✳ Tip

Seeing the most stressed word
Help students to put the stress on the right word by writing this word on the board in CAPITALS.

Listening

Taking a reservation by telephone

- 🎧 As well as predicting the order, students can also predict the questions. Get students to focus on the gist task in **1** and not try to complete the form until **2**.

Item	Order	Information
Surname	7	Steinmetz
Room type	4	twin
Arrival date	1	Monday 12
Departure date	2	Thursday 15
Adults	3	2
# Rooms	5	1
Smoking / Non-smoking	6	Non-smoking
Card type	9	Mastercard
Credit card #	8	4922 6481 6262 3383
Name (on card)	10	Barbara Steinmetz
Expiry date	11	August 2008

Pronunciation

- This activity raises students' awareness of *sentence stress*. Incorrect sentence stress can badly affect the speaker's intelligibility.

- 🎧 Get students to listen to the four phrases in **1**, then check the answers. Encourage students to look at the listening script for the dialogue (p.132) when answering **2**. Play the dialogue and then check the answers.

- In **3**, practise by back-chaining, e.g. say *NAME is it, please?*, then *What NAME is it, please?*, or *SPELL that, please?*, and then *Could you SPELL that, please?*

1 1 help   2 single   3 twin   4 singles
2 1 name   2 spell   3 number   4 Visa   5 expiry

Customer care

Smile on the phone

- Ask students if they have had any good / bad experiences of telephoning a company. Was the person rude / miserable, friendly, over-friendly? Carry out the experiment. You can work in threes with one student appointed as an observer – in order to prove how effective this technique is.

Speaking

Taking a telephone booking

- Allow students to read through the script for the listening on p.66 first (p.132). Revise some of the questions that might be asked. Focus your attention on stress and rhythm when correcting / praising.

Checklist, Key words, Next stop

- See suggestions on p.5. Remind students about transferring vocabulary into their Personal Learning Dictionaries.

8 Marketing and promotion

Background

Marketing is essential for the success of both private companies and public organizations. Its purpose is to ensure that the right product is created and made available to the right people. Good marketing is beneficial both for the company / organization creating a product, and for the people who buy it.

The *marketing process* is central to all marketing, and involves four steps:

- identification of the customer's needs / wants
- development of suitable products and services
- promotion of the products and services
- monitoring and evaluation.

The first of these involves *market research*. This tells companies their customers' ages, income levels, interests, needs, satisfaction with current products, etc.

The next step, the development of products and services, uses a *SWOT analysis*. The letters stand for:

- **S**trengths. This refers to the good points of the product you want to market. If a resort hotel has a private beach, but the other hotels in the same area do not, the beach is one of the hotel's strengths.
- **W**eaknesses. Poor roads and communications would be considered a weakness for most types of tourism.
- **O**pportunities are the ways a business can expand or improve its services. If a region signs an agreement with a low-cost airline, this is an opportunity for local tourism suppliers like hoteliers.
- **T**hreats are products or policies that might affect your business negatively. If a competitor offers a holiday very similar to one you sell, but at a lower price, this is a threat.

Using a SWOT analysis, tourism managers can create a *product* that is better than that of their competitors. The product, however, is only one of four aspects of what is called the marketing mix. These are often referred to as *the four Ps*, and consist of product, price, place, and promotion.

Price is a crucial part of the mix, but getting the price right for a particular product is a very complex business. *Place* refers both to the location of the holiday itself, and to how the product is made available to the public. For example, deciding to sell a product directly to the client or through a travel agency is an issue of place.

Promotion in tourism uses a range of promotional techniques, including:

- *Advertising* – adverts on TV, the radio, in magazines and newspapers, on the Internet, etc.
- *Direct marketing* – sending letters or emails to people whose addresses a company has on its database. Direct mailing means you only contact the people most likely to buy your product.
- *Personal selling* – this is vital to the success of a travel agency, and is the sale through talking face-to-face with the customer.
- *Public relations* – paying travel journalists to use one of your products and then write about it; making sure that all of the staff of a company that come into direct contact with the public project a good image of the company.
- *Sales promotion* – a range of activities (discounts, competitions, brochures, exhibitions, free gifts, exhibitions, price cuts, etc.) all designed to stimulate short-term demand for a product.

✳ Tip

Real adverts
Find examples of real travel and tourism adverts and bring them in. They will make a good visual display, as well as providing source material for reference throughout the unit.

Take off

- Students work in groups to think of ideas. Encourage them to be as wide-ranging as possible in their ideas for **2**.
- They can refer to real advertisements they know.

Reading
What is marketing?

- Students discuss the statements in **1** in pairs, then read to find the specific information.
- Report back on **2** before moving on to **3** and **4**.

- For **5**, if you have a class where students get on with each other, you can also ask them to nominate others students who would be good at different stages.

> **2** 1 F   2 T   3 F   4 T
> **3** 1 stage 2   2 stage 4   3 stage 1
> **4** 1 stage 2   3 stage 3

Vocabulary
Marketing terminology

- Students can either work in pairs or individually on this.

- You can work on parts of speech – noun, adjective, verb forms – if you want, e.g. *advertise – advertisement, know – knowledge*.

> 2 g   3 d   4 e   5 f   6 i   7 b   8 a   9 h

✚ Additional activity
(stronger students)
Introduce other related verb patterns, e.g.
make sb do sth
allow sb to do sth
be prepared to do sth.
Students can research their meaning and grammatical behaviour in the English–English dictionary.

Language spot
Verb patterns

- Remind students about the way an English–English dictionary works and how useful it can be in understanding a word.

- Help students with the dictionary notation (*sb, sth*, etc.) and show them where the key in their dictionary is.

- In particular, focus on the example sentence and show how it illustrates the grammatical patterns associated with the word.

- Students check answers in pairs before reporting back.

> **3** 1 a   2 c
> **4** 1 hope   2 gear   3 hope   4 let   5 lets   6 gear

Customer care
Learn from your customers

- Ask students if they have ever completed a customer feedback form. What was the situation? Did they enjoy doing it? Did they find it useful? What do they think the company did with it?

- Students work in groups to brainstorm ideas on areas to find out about.

✚ Additional activity
(all levels)
Students write their own Top Ten for a city they know well. It could be made into a game with students reading out one or two of their Top Ten attractions and the other students having to guess 'where in the world' it is.

Where in the world?

- After some general discussion about Newcastle and Gateshead from the photos, allow students to go where their interest takes them on the page. Be available to answer any questions they have.

- Time spent exploring this page will help when it comes to the following listening (and other activities later in the unit).

- **3** can be discussed in pairs or groups.

> **2** a 2 b 5 c 6 d 1

Listening
Analysing your product

- Write *S – W – O – T* in the four quarters of the board. Write *strengths,* then help the students to decide what the other letters stand for.

- Before looking at the table, get students to think about the SWOT for NewcastleGateshead based on the *Where in the world?* article.

- 🎧 Get students to focus on the gist question in **2** and the detail question in **3**, comparing answers in pairs after each listening before reporting back.

> **2** 1st S, 2nd O, 3rd T, 4th W
> **3** Strengths: 1, 2, 4   Opportunities: 1, 3
>   Weaknesses: 1, 4   Threats: 2

Speaking
Do you SWOT?

- Keep the initial stage very general – i.e. cities in general, not specific cities. Try to cover some of the areas that come up in **2**.

- Give students plenty of time to read through their information, and help with any vocabulary and pronunciation issues.

Top margin

- Get students to read through and then discuss. Do any of the facts seem surprising? Do any of the figures seem high or low?

Listening
Promotion in tourism

- This is quite a difficult listening, so it is important to spend some time familiarizing students with the content via the diagram and pre-teaching vocabulary (*create, stimulate, remind, competitor, operate,* and the four Ps).

- Read through the questions and predict answers to **3** and **4**.

- 🎧 Pause the recording from time to time if you feel it is appropriate.

> **2** 1 Price   4 Direct
>   2 Place   5 Personal selling
>   3 Promotion
> **3** 1, 2, and 3
> **4** 1 F   2 F   3 T   4 F

Find out

- Discuss **1** in small groups. Get the groups to assign specific tasks to each group member (e.g. one to research public sector offices, one to look at private sector associations, etc.). Use the website addresses collected earlier to help.

- Report back in a later lesson.

Pronunciation

- Let students work in pairs on **1**, then check the answers.

- For **3**, students should cover the words and use only the transcriptions.

- ⌒ As students hear each word in **4**, invite them to comment on words or sounds that they find surprising or different to their expectations.

- In **5**, encourage them to express their own opinions, and avoid giving the idea that one particular word is the hardest / easiest.

> ⚿
> **1** 1 d   2 f   3 j   4 b   5 k   6 a   7 g   8 h   9 e   10 i   11 c

✱ Tip

Nouns as adjectives
Luxury is usually a noun, but can often be used as an adjective in preference to *luxurious*.

Vocabulary

The language of advertising

- Write the sentence *Rome is a nice city* on the board. Ask students to suggest alternatives for *nice*.

- Do **1** to **3** in open class. Work in pairs for **4** and **5**, reporting back after each activity.

> ⚿
> **1** 1 c   2 b   3 d   4 a
> **4** 1 f,m   2 d,i   3 c,j   4 e,k   5 h,l   6 a,g   7 b,n
> **5**
> 1 historic   3 innovative   5 economical
> 2 low-cost   4 exclusive   6 Gorgeous

➕ Additional activity

(stronger students)
Write up a critical report on tourism promotion in the area, including a classification of promotional material and a SWOT analysis of strategies being used, etc.

Writing

Adverts

- Students brainstorm ideas in pairs or small groups.

- They should then look at some example websites and note down features that they like.

- Students are not expected to be web designers, but it is quite fun and useful to mock them up as authentically as possible.

Reading
Promotional techniques

- Check students understand the meaning of the promotion techniques in **1**. Students can either read all the campaigns to find the answers (stronger students), or be assigned one of the campaigns to read and then report back on to their groups (weaker students).

- In **2**, judge each of the campaigns in groups.

> **O─╖**
>
> North-east England – competition
> Hong Kong – discounted prices
> Rio de Janeiro – displays and exhibitions
> Languedoc – display / posters

Language spot
Superlatives

- If necessary, refer back to the work on comparatives in Unit 6.

> **O─╖**
>
> **1** 1 cheapest   2 highest   3 most original

Speaking
Presenting a campaign

- This activity pulls together many of the themes of the unit. It could take place over a series of lessons.

- Encourage students to use visuals and be as imaginative as possible in their presentations.

- Keep all the displays for a class exhibition or for the course portfolio.

➕ Additional activity
(weaker students)
Get students to write a series of news headlines only – i.e. not the whole text. Other students can ask questions about the stories behind the headlines.

Writing
Promotional campaign news

- Make this a collaborative effort with different students producing different parts of the news items for the web page.

- Alternatively you can make this into an individual course assignment, as it brings together many of the themes of the unit.

Checklist, Key words, Next stop

- See suggestions on p.5. Remind students about transferring vocabulary into their Personal Learning Dictionaries.

9 The airline industry

Background

It is possible that no single factor has changed tourism as much as the introduction of air travel, and in particular the introduction of commercial jet aircraft in the 1950s. Initially, the airline industry was built around a limited number of airlines. All activity was strictly regulated by the international air authorities, particularly IATA (the International Air Transport Association), which represents more than 80% of the world's major airlines. Today the industry is divided into:

● *Traditional* airlines – such as KLM or Qantas. In countries where the main airline is or was publicly owned, the company is known as the *flag carrier*. This is the case with British Airways and the UK.

● *Low-cost* airlines – these offer scheduled flights but use certain strategies to keep seat costs low. These include
  – use of the Internet for paperless ticketing
  – avoidance of sales through travel agents leading to savings in commissions
  – minimum time for the aircraft on the ground to achieve more flights per day
  – concentration on short- and medium-haul flights to maximize the number of flights per day
  – use of only one type of aircraft to reduce maintenance costs
  – hiring of fully qualified pilots, passenger cabin crew, and ground staff to avoid training costs.

Within the industry, each airline is identified by a *code* consisting of two or three letters, e.g. IB for Iberia or EZY for easyJet. *Code sharing* is a recent practice through which an airline sells seats, under its own name, on another airline's flight.

● *Scheduled flights* operate on a specific route at fixed times that have been published in timetables. Even if the plane is empty, a scheduled flight must take off. Flights are classed as short-, medium-, or long-haul.

● *Charter flights* run on a route and at a time chosen by the company or person that hires the aircraft. Tour operators use charter flights for most package holidays. Charter flights are inevitably fuller than scheduled flights, making the cost of each seat lower.

Like airlines, airports are also given a code, of three letters. MAD is Madrid, and STN is London Stansted. Airports have grown with the increase in air travel, and many major cities have more than one airport. Larger airports often have more than one *terminal*.

A *gateway airport* provides international passengers with access to a country. Frankfurt, for example, is Germany's major gateway airport. In contrast, a *hub airport* is one that a specific airline uses to distribute its flights to other airports in the same country. Atlanta is the hub for Delta airlines in the USA.

➕ Additional activity

(all levels)
For an active warmer, give each of the students one of the words or phrases (double up or divide into groups if necessary). They stand in the order they think they should be and then move around as they listen to check. This method has the added advantage of encouraging the students to pronounce the words and phrases.

✳ Tip

Concept check questions
To check students really understand the meaning of words, ask concept check questions. For example: *What do you give the official when you check in? What does the official give you? What is the opposite of taking off (or window seat)?*

Take off

● 🎧 Look at the pictures and see how much vocabulary students can come up with. Do **1** and **2** in pairs, then listen (**3**) to check.

🔑		
1 check-in (g)	4 passenger cabin crew (c)	7 cruise (a)
2 security control (f)	5 taxi (d)	8 landing (b)
3 boarding card (h)	6 take-off (e)	

Listening
The ups and downs of flying

● 🎧 Check students understand the vocabulary in the table before listening.

● 🎧 In **3**, students can try to guess the missing words before listening again.

O—
1

	Isabel	Alexi	Millie	Gustavo
Travelling to and from airports	✓			
Checking in		✗		
Going through security			✗	
Waiting to embark				–
Boarding when you ...		✗		
Taking off			✓	
A window seat				✓
Landing	✓			
Waiting for your luggage				✗
Travel delays			✗	

3

1	love travelling	4	really love it	7	don't mind
2	don't mind	5	hate	8	hate waiting
3	quite like	6	really hate		

✱ Tip

Ranking exercises

Sometimes it can help increase communication if the items in a ranking exercise like this are written on pieces of paper which students then have to physically move. Because students will tend to hold on to the pieces of paper, they will need to be asked to put them in a place or to suggest where they go.

Language spot
'like' or 'dislike'

- Work in pairs or small groups on **1**. **2** can be discussed in open class.

- **3** can be done in pairs, or you can make it a mingling activity, with students going round the class asking about likes and dislikes.

O—
1 really love – love – like – quite like – don't mind – don't like – really don't like – hate – really hate
2 *really like* is more positive

✱ Tip

Using dictionaries effectively

To encourage the effective (and communicative) use of dictionaries, it is a good idea in activities like this to nominate one student per four or five to be the 'dictionary holder': the other students consult him or her if they want to check something in the dictionary. (It also means you don't have to carry so many dictionaries into the class!)

Vocabulary
Air travel

- Students can work through **1–4** on their own and then check with a partner before reporting back. Allow the use of English–English dictionaries if you want (see tip).

- In **4**, stronger students can use other forms of the verbs – e.g. past tenses.

O—
1 1 flight 2 flying 3 fly
2 fly = verb, flight = noun describing a particular journey, flying = noun (or gerund) describing air travel in general (and also present participle).
3 1 departure   3 check in   5 land / take off
    2 arrivals   4 take-off   6 boarding

Top margin

- Ask students if they think air travel is dangerous, and if accident rates have increased or decreased in recent years.

- Get them to read the fact to find out, and also report back on the information on fuel emissions.

Additional activity
(weaker students)
Give out a list of jumbled questions and answers (including the ones in **3**), and get students to match them and locate exactly where in the text the answers are given.

Reading
Tourism and air travel

- Encourage students to make predictions about the article in **1**. Use their ideas to bring out vocabulary to pre-teach or check – e.g. *jet aircraft, codes, scheduled, long-haul / short-haul, security, pollution*.

- Get students to read through the questions in **3** and **4** and check they understand them before reading. Discuss answers in pairs before reporting back to class.

> **O─**
> **2** 2
> **3** a 1.5 billion   b 80   c 3
> **4 Possible answers**
> 1 it's possible to travel to faraway places quickly; it transports lots of people; it employs lots of people
> 2 people get frightened; security worries; pollution (carbon emissions)

Find out

- Students will need to be selective in choosing exactly which websites to help them answer the questions. All of this is extremely useful for developing their wider tourism and research skills, but you may want to research some particular sites to recommend to your students before you set the task.

Pronunciation

- Model one or two names and codes in **1**.

- ⌒ Play the recording in **2**, checking and correcting the pronunciation of /t/ and /d/ only. Monitor **3** and **4** and assist as necessary.

Speaking
The air travel route map

- Give students time to browse the map, then say the name of a country and ask for the corresponding term. After five or six names, invert the process and say some terms, seeking the country names.

- Check the pronunciation of the different terms as you move around the class. Finish by checking all the answers in open class.

- For **2**, divide the class into teams. Allow time for students to study the definitions before they compete, helping as necessary. For **3**, point out that it is important to be able to describe technical terms using your own words.

> **⊶**
> | | |
> |---|---|
> | Hub, Baggage = Canada | First class = Spain |
> | Connecting flight = the USA | Code sharing = Ivory Coast |
> | Direct flight = Cuba | Scheduled airline = Mozambique |
> | Frequent flyer programme, | Gateway airport = South Africa |
> | Terminal = Brazil | RTW = South Korea |
> | Transit = Argentina | Non-stop flight = China |
> | Overbooking = Iceland | Stopover = Burma |
> | Return trip = Finland | Fly/Drive package = India |
> | Air ticket = Russia | Open-jaw trip = Australia |
> | Carrier code = Germany | |

✳ Tip

Checking in pairs

Apart from giving the opportunity for more communication between the students (provided it is in English), one reason for getting students to check their answers to a listening in pairs before reporting back or listening again, is so that you can go round the class and see how well they have done. You can thus gauge whether they need to hear the listening again, if you need to pause it, or if you can move on.

Listening
Low-cost or traditional?

- Write *low-cost* and *traditional* on the board. Divide each column into 'advantages' and 'disadvantages' and elicit ideas from the students. If necessary, give prompts such as: *booking, cost, check-in, comfort, staff.*

- In pairs, students do **1** and then report back. Make sure that all the important vocabulary from the listening has been covered.

- 🎧 Before doing **2**, point out that the characteristics are not in the order they hear them, and that not all of them are mentioned.

- Pairs check answers after the first listening – they may need to hear it again. Report back in open class. Discuss **3** and **4** in open class as well.

> **⊶**
> **2** | | | |
> |---|---|---|
> | 1 not mentioned | 4 traditional | 7 not mentioned |
> | 2 low-cost | 5 traditional | 8 traditional |
> | 3 traditional | 6 not mentioned | |

➕ Additional activity

(weaker students)

As the article might be quite long for some students, you can divide the class into two groups: one to find out as much as they can about traditional airlines, and to ignore any information on low-cost; the other to do the reverse. Students from each group then pair up to answer the questions collaboratively.

Reading
Revolution in the skies

- Focus attention on the logos and do **1** and **2**.

- Spend plenty of time on **3**, as it will generate interest in the text and allow you to pre-teach the important vocabulary. The same is true for the statements in **4**, which students can be asked to predict before reading.

> **⊶**
> **1** Ryanair, easyJet, and Buzz (which is now owned by Ryanair).
> **2** They are all low-cost airlines.
> **4** 1 b   2 a   3 a   4 b   5 b   6 a   7 c   8 b   9 c

➕ Additional activity

(weaker students)

Write down all the parts of the lexical items that fit in the gaps on separate pieces of paper (e.g. LOW – COST – CARRIER) and jumble them up. Students use the pieces of paper to fill the gaps.

Vocabulary
Low-cost carriers

- Students work in pairs and report back to the whole class.

> **⊶**
> | | | |
> |---|---|---|
> | 1 budget airline | 4 Low-cost carriers | 6 landing, take-off charges |
> | 2 stopover | 5 paperless ticketing | 7 turnaround time |
> | 3 short-haul | | |

➕ **Additional activity**

(stronger students)

Get students to look back through the article and find other examples of collocations – e.g. *domestic flights, cabin crew, intercontinental routes.*

Writing
Producing a questionnaire

● Discuss the advantages of multiple-choice questions – e.g. *easier to complete, easier to correlate results.* Get students to work in pairs on the questions to ask, ensuring grammatical accuracy and a good use of multiple-choice where appropriate. They can write the final version of the questionnaire for homework.

Language spot
Asking questions politely

● Write *How old are you?* on the board, and point out the importance of asking such a question politely and sensitively. Elicit or give the polite indirect form – *Can I ask you how old you are?* Point out that (a) there are other ways of starting the question – *Could you tell me ...* or *Would you mind telling me ...,* and (b) the word order in the main question part is different from a direct question (because the question inversion takes place in the polite part). Point out the use of *if* in 'yes / no' questions – use an example like: *Do you speak English? / Could you tell me **if** you speak English?*

● 🎧 Drill the indirect questions to ensure polite intonation and clarity.

>
>
> **2** 1 Would you mind answering a couple of questions about air travel?
> 2 Could I ask you how often you fly?
> 3 Can I ask you if you use low-cost airlines at all?

Customer care
Questionnaire tactics

● As well as matching the three statements in **1**, get them to think of other expressions they might hear for the pieces of advice.

It's my job

● After they have looked at the four statements, let students read about Javier.

● Check the answers. Ask the class if they agree with Javier, especially about the secret to working in tourism.

>
>
> 1 F   2 F   3 T   4 T

Checklist, Key words, Next stop

● See suggestions on p.5. Remind students about transferring vocabulary into their Personal Learning Dictionaries.

10 Holidays with a difference

Background

One of the most revealing moments for students of tourism when they go to their first trade fair is discovering the enormous range of holidays on offer. Even today, many people associate tourism with lying on a beach near a warm sea. The reality is quite different, and more and more tour operators, large and small, try to tailor their products to the public's diverse tastes.

The classic three Ss holiday (sea, sand, and sun) still dominates the industry, but many tourists today seek something different. This unit concentrates on four broad classes of alternative holiday. These are:

Adventure and action. Here the emphasis is on the tourist's active participation. Qualified instructors are present at all times in order to guarantee the clients' safety. The *Karakoram Experience* text describes holidays of this type. This type of holiday can also be taken in the absence of instructors by a group of friends doing their own organization, as is the case of the mountaineer interviewed in the listening on p.86.

There are many definitions of **ecotourism** but all involve
● responsible travel to a natural area

● the conservation of the environment visited
● sustaining the well-being of the local people.
Where in the world? describes an increasingly popular ecotourism destination – Antarctica.

As a result of the stress of modern living, tourists are increasingly seeking relaxation in a range of holidays that can be classed as **escape and enlightenment**. Escape can come through a stay in a spa, a health farm, or some similar place where it is possible to get away from the urgency and tension of life today. Enlightenment can come directly through the practice of activities such as yoga and meditation, or indirectly through the discovery of self often made by people on pilgrimages such as the Camino de Santiago in Northern Spain.

There have been **cultural and heritage** holidays since the beginnings of modern tourism and the Grand Tour of Europe undertaken by the upper classes in the 18th century. Nowadays such holidays involve anything in which the purpose of the visit is increased knowledge and understanding of other people and their culture. But as the text on Mongolia suggests, it is important to be aware of how to behave when visiting other cultures.

* Tip
Personalization
Bring your own personal experiences as a tourist and a traveller to the classroom – e.g. anecdotes, holiday snaps, etc. Students usually love to hear about what their teachers do / have done outside the class.

➕ Additional activity
(weaker students)
Ask students just to listen for one (or two) of the categories.

Take off
● Use the advertisement to establish the contrast between 'traditional' holidays and 'holidays with a difference'. Do **1** in pairs. Ask students for their experiences in **2**, and describe some of your own.

Listening
At the trade fair

● Students do **1** and **2** in pairs. Use the pictures to pre-teach new words.
● 🎧 Students discuss their answers to **3** and **4** in pairs and then report back.

2 1 diving, volcanoes, white-water rafting, biking, the Caribbean, cattle ranch, Costa Rica, horse riding
2 ecosystem, expedition, Antarctica, sea-life
3 pilgrimage, Mexico, spa and health resorts, India
4 working farm, gastronomic week, France
4 1 Costa Rica 3 Seven Holy Cities of India
2 Antarctica expedition 4 France gastronomic week

Vocabulary
Different holiday types

- **1** and **3** can be done in pairs; **2** and **4** can be discussed in open class.

> **1** 1 b, d, e, k, n   2 c, h, p   3 i, l, m   4 a, f, g, j, o
> **3** cliff jumping   jet-skiing   hang-gliding
>   heli-skiing   bungee jumping   windsurfing
>   snowboarding   horse riding   camel riding
>   whale-watching   mountain biking   birdwatching
>   hillwalking   scuba-diving   white-water rafting
>   skateboarding   water-skiing

✚ Additional activity
(all levels)
This unit introduces many different and less well-known destinations, e.g. Peru, Lapland, Kyrgyzstan, Bolivia, Tajikistan, Mongolia. Early on in the unit give each student one of these places to research and find out about. Then, when the place is mentioned in the course of the unit, the student can report on it as 'class expert'.

Reading
The Karakoram Experience

- Use a world map to locate the places mentioned in the reading. Students work in pairs and then report back to class.

> **1** The founders enjoyed travelling in the Karakoram Mountains.
> **2** horse riding, rafting, biking, trekking, ski touring, snowshoe hiking, fishing, wildlife adventures
> **3** mountains, jungle, (frozen) lake, beaches
> **4** more adventurous, people interested in something different

Listening
Interview with a mountaineer

- 🎧 Get students to predict the best and worst experiences of being a mountaineer. Also ask them what tourist services a mountaineer would use. Use both questions to pre-teach new vocabulary. Students read through **1** and **2** before listening, and then compare answers in pairs.

> **1** 1 13   5 when friends have been killed in accidents
>   2 Kyrgyzstan, Tajikistan   6 on the top of mountains with friends, or
>   3 a, c   back at base camp
>   4 6,400 m
> **2** 1 did / start   5 do / tour company
>   2 about / did /do   6 you've climbed
>   3 tour company / do it yourself 7 ever been
>   4 did you   8 ever / of giving up

✱ Tip
Traditional v practical grammar
Students may be tired of doing 'traditional' grammar. However, point out that the grammar covered in this course is only presented if it is practical and needed in the job, and that consequently it may be presented slightly differently than in their 'general English' courses. For example, here we are more interested in producing the question form, because this is going to be more relevant for a tourism provider.

Language spot
Asking and talking about experience

- Use the examples to explain the difference between general experience (Present Perfect) and specific occasions in the past (Past Simple).
- In **2**, see who can find the examples in the listening extract first.
- Students do **3** in pairs and then report back – one student asking the question, the other providing a possible answer.

> **O┰**
> **1** I've been to ... = Present Perfect; we used a ... = Past Simple
> **2** Present Perfect: What's the highest mountain you've climbed? / Have you ever been frightened? / Have you ever thought of giving up?
> Past Simple: When did you start mountain climbing? / What about expedition mountaineering? When did you do that? / How did you find a suitable company?
> **3** 1 e,f   2 a,b,c,d   3 d,g   4 j   5 e,f   6 g,i,k

Top margin

- Ask students what they understand by the term *ecotourism*, and to come up with some specific examples. Look at the definition and the quotes. Do they agree with the quotes? To some extent they contradict each other, so students should decide which one they agree with most.

- Ask them if there is one place in the world they would leave alone.

Speaking

Have you ever ...?

- Identify the activities in the pictures and check pronunciation. Model one of the dialogues in open class, before pairs do **1**. For **2**, students can choose any activities mentioned in the unit so far. They mingle, noting down what they find out, and using freer language to persuade the others to do it. Discuss their general findings in open class.

Pronunciation

✳ Tip

Monolingual classes
Ignore these activities if you work with a monolingual group that can pronounce all three sounds well.

- 🎧 Do **1**. In **2**, get students to look at you and at each other while they become familiar with the mouth positions. After **4**, get students to produce sentences containing as many /b/, /v/, and /w/ sounds as they can.

> **O┰**
> **1** 1 vest   3 vine   5 best
>   2 berry   4 whale   6 veil

Top margin

- Relate the facts and percentages to the language of trends practised in Unit 4 and the idea of 'old' and 'new' tourism.

➕ Additional activity

(all levels)
To get more practice at making questions – and to help with the *Speaking* activity that follows – get students to read the text and make questions based on it (e.g. *How many scientists live there in the summer?*). Their partner has to answer the questions without looking at the text.

Where in the world?

- Use the pictures to bring out any relevant vocabulary. Elicit on to the board: *Things we know*, *Things we're not sure about*, and *Things we'd like to know* about Antarctica. Let students read the article at their own pace to find the answers, and any other information that interests them.

✛ Additional activity

(stronger students)
Carry out the role-play as a phone conversation, with students sitting back-to-back.

Speaking
Questions on Antarctica

- Give students plenty of time to read through their information files.

Reading
Cultural differences

- Brainstorm areas where there can be intercultural differences and misunderstandings for tourists. Some standard ideas might be: *greeting, queuing, eating in restaurants, going to someone's house, taking photos.*

- Brainstorm what the students know about Mongolia. Get students to read the fact file. Did they discover anything they didn't know? Ask what cultural differences there might be.

- In pairs or groups, do **1**. Encourage as much debate and disagreement as possible. Check answers in **2**. Students form new groups to do **3**.

Writing
Cultural tips

- Get students in groups to brainstorm ideas for each of the categories. They can write the 'tips' for homework. Compare the different lists in class, then try to find an authentic English-language list of tips for the students' countries – e.g. from the Internet.

✱ Tip

Culture files

Get students to build up 'culture files' for a few countries that they are interested in. These can be expanded into more far-reaching 'fact files', but the emphasis should be on cultural differences and cultural tips for tourists.

✱ Tip

Search engines

One way to help students learn and retain new vocabulary, particularly unusual words, is to get them to type the lexical set into a search engine plus the name of a place (e.g. yoga, massage, t'ai chi, shiatsu, meditation, Scotland). This will automatically produce texts with the vocabulary authentically located. It also helps with spelling practice.

Find out

- Get students to choose a country they are interested in. (If you have used the Additional activity idea for the Karakoram Experience reading, then they can find out about the country they were assigned there.)

Vocabulary
Escape and enlightenment holidays

- Use the pictures to identify the vocabulary. **1** and **2** can be done in open class. Do **3** in pairs. Note that none of the words in **1** appear in the Camino de Santiago description. You may want to point this out and get stronger students to predict the words that might appear.

- Still in pairs, read through one of the brochure descriptions, helping each other with vocabulary and making notes for **4** if necessary. Divide into new groups of three for **4** and **5**.

O━
1 a aromatherapy   d spa
   b yoga / meditation   e anti-aging treatment
   c t'ai chi
2 Possible answers
spa, retreat
spa: massage, aromatherapy, shiatsu, anti-aging treatment
retreat: meditation, t'ai chi, yoga
3
  1 spa, retreat, yoga, hikes, massage, aromatherapy, anti-aging treatment
  2 none
  3 yoga, retreat, meditation, t'ai chi, hiking, shiatsu

Language spot
Describing service provision

● In groups of three, students refer back to the descriptions to find further examples for **1**. **2** can be done individually.

O─

1 **Possible answers**
1 (It) **boasts** a perfect mountain climate. (A)
Rio Caliente **provides** the ideal secluded location for the spa-goer ... (A)
It **provides** a quiet and beautiful setting for retreats. (C)
These retreats **provide** an excellent introduction to ... (C)
2 **You can choose** the section that passes through ... (B)
You can start at any point along the route. (B)
You can learn to meditate... (C)
This **can help you develop** clarity, ... (C)
3 Your luggage **is moved** ahead each day ... (B)
You **are accommodated** in comfortable small hotels ... (B)
The classes **are taught** from basic principles ... (C)
4 **Recharge** your spirit and your imagination. **Recharge** your body and soul. **Come** to Rio Caliente! (A)
Book early as these retreats are very popular. (C)
2 1 offers / provides   2 You can   3 You can   4 is held   5 Book

Customer care
Ability and suitability

● In small groups or open class, discuss the four questions.

O─

Possible answers
3 fill in forms and questionnaires about health and previous experience, provide a short trial activity
4 if they are too young, have health problems, or if they are under the influence of alcohol or drugs

✚ Additional activity
(all levels)
Ask the class to decide on a 'holiday with a difference' for you.

Speaking
Tourist types and holiday types

● After **1**, collect in the pieces of paper, shuffle them up and redistribute to the groups. When students are working on **2**, encourage them to argue and disagree. Don't let them use the same holiday type more than once.

Checklist, Key words, Next stop

● See suggestions on p.5. Remind students about transferring vocabulary into their Personal Learning Dictionaries.

11 Reservations and sales

Background

Taking a booking is one of the stages in the sales process featured in Unit 5. Each agency has a procedure for its sales consultants to follow. The points in the memo on p.92 are common to most package holiday bookings. A fixed booking procedure

- guarantees that key information is correctly recorded
- avoids the need to contact the client later for information not obtained when he / she was in the agency
- avoids problems arising from incorrect information.

In a travel agency a typical booking involves:

- completion of the booking form
- payment of a deposit – typically a fixed amount per person, but sometimes a fixed percentage of the total cost
- transfer of the booking information to the tour operator or service provider in order to check availability
- issue of a confirmation note by the tour operator
- payment of the balance (the rest of the cost of the holiday), usually six to eight weeks before departure.

Tourism professionals often refer to

- **Computer Reservation Systems** (CRS). These originated in the 1950s and initially were restricted to internal use in airlines. The first was SABRE (**S**emi-**A**utomatic **B**usiness **R**esearch **E**nvironment), an American Airlines development in 1959. On seeing the value of CRSs, the airlines opened up their systems to other airlines and to recognized travel agencies. As a result, sales consultants could access information about availability of flights offered by more than one company, and they could do this at the same time as they were taking a booking.
- **Global Distribution Systems** (GDS). More recently, CRSs have begun to carry a wide range of tourism products and services (flights, rooms, car hire, etc.).
- **Gateways**. Direct access to GDSs is costly and requires a licence that only a travel agent can afford. In order to make travel reservations available directly to the public, special computer programmes (gateways) are used. These are accessed by the public through the Internet.

GDSs all use abbreviations for the information they present on screen to sales consultants in travel agencies. The reading on p.95 gives students some of the most common codes and abbreviations for air tickets.

Take off

- If possible, bring in some realia, e.g. your own passport. Students identify the pictures (and the realia) in pairs and answer **1** and **2**. For **3**, start with an anecdote of your own (invented if necessary), and then get students to discuss their own experiences. This activity will recycle *Have you ever?* and Past Simple from Unit 10.

Additional activity

(stronger students)
To get some extra practice at question-forming, ask students to make questions for each of the items on the list.

✱ Tip

Number warmers

There are a lot of numbers and dates involved in this unit. To encourage familiarity and fluency start each lesson with a 'number warmer', for example:

- Students get in order of their birthdays (a mingling activity).
- Students write three numbers or dates that are personally important to them (e.g. a phone number or an anniversary) and tell their partner about them.
- Bingo with dates and numbers.

Reading

Holiday bookings – getting the right information

- For **1**, brainstorm one or two ideas in open class first and then get students to think of others in pairs. Do **2** to check. Answer **3** in open class, and get pairs to work on **4**.

> **3** 'et cetera' (and other things)
> **4** a 13, b 8, c 11, d 3, e 10, f 14, g 12

Listening

Taking a booking

- 🎧 As this is quite a long listening, you may want to break it into chunks. Spend time before the listening discussing the possible answers. Students compare answers in pairs after each listening.

➕ Additional activity

(all levels)

Email address dictation. Check students are familiar with the pronunciation of email address symbols (at, dot, hyphen, underscore). Read out some email addresses for students to copy down.

Oⁿ

1 first name   Susan
  address   64 Bridge Lane, Lazenthorpe
  tel no   0774 797 9799
  email   venables.s-r@hotmail.com
  no of people   2
  outward journey   21/9
  return journey   11/10
  meal basis   half board
  method of payment   credit card
  deposit details   £240
3 double-check all the details
4 within the next two weeks; check the details and let the travel agent
  know if there are any mistakes

➕ Additional activity

(weaker students)

Rather than choose holidays from Unit 10, weaker students can read the script from the listening, writing down basic information from each role to serve as 'reminders'. They then reconstruct the dialogue from these 'reminders'.

Speaking

Have you decided where to go?

- Before dividing into pairs of sales consultants and clients, let students prepare with others who have the same role. For **3**, when roles are reversed, students can go straight into their paired roles. At the end, get one or two pairs to act out their role-play in front of the class. Other students comment.

Writing

Confirming a booking

- This can be done as homework.

Reading

Computer reservation systems

- Discuss **1** and **2** in open class. Ask students if they have met these terms in other subjects they are studying. Students compare answers to **3** in pairs.

Oⁿ

1 CRS = Computer / Computerized Reservations System
  GDS = Global Distribution System
2 dictionary, specialist dictionary, internet search engine
3 1 T 2 T 3 F 4 T 5 F 6 T

Vocabulary

Reservation systems for tourism

- Before answering the questions, get students to locate each of the words in the text so that they are looking for the meaning of the word in context.

Oⁿ

1 c 2 b 3 a 4 b

Listening
The origin of CRSs

- 🎧 Pairs can compare answers between listenings. At the end, students can read through the script.

System	SABRE	Amadeus	Galileo
Created by	American Airlines and IBM	Air France, Iberia, Scandinavian Airlines, Lufthansa	British Airways, KLM, Swissair, Alitalia
Created in	1959	1987	1993
Market share	30%	30%	25%

2 created in 1990 by Delta, Northwest Airlines, TWA, market share 15%

Top margin

- Use the first fact to discuss the role of the Internet in tourism in general, and how tourism professionals would work without the Internet. For the second fact, ask the students why the hotel website booking is cheaper than the travel agent and GDS. Are there any advantages to it?

Find out

- Students visit a local travel agency in pairs with prepared questions. Reporting back can be done within groups of four or six students, who then prepare a summary of their findings.

Reading
Abbreviations and codes

- Allow students time to look at the printout and see if they recognize any words, abbreviations, or dates. Work in pairs to answer **1** and **2**.

1 1 26 June 3 no – only one flight number and date
    2 €270 4 one-way

2	1 ADT	3 AL	5 E	7 JUN	9 NRF	11 SU
	2 ADV	4 CK	6 FTC	8 MIN	10 PTC	12 TRF

Customer care
Putting on the pressure

- Get students to discuss in groups which statement they agree with most, then work on **2** in pairs.

➕ Additional activity
(all levels)
Play 'abbreviation scrabble'. Take as many scrabble tiles as you can. Give out seven to each player (in groups of five or six – although it will depend on how many tiles you have). They take turns to make tourism abbreviations, not just from this unit but other topics as well (e.g. flight codes and airport codes). They must be able to say what they are. Players take new tiles as in ordinary scrabble (but there is no board). For a bit of fun, you can also allow them to invent their own abbreviations, provided it has a tourism theme (e.g. FANAD = Flight Attendant Needs A Drink).

✚ Additional activity
(stronger students)
Students produce a single statement combining the aspects of A and B that they agree with.

✚ Additional activity
(all levels)
Extend **3** into a 'consequences' activity. Each student starts a story chain by writing a tourist problem on the top of a sheet of paper (e.g. *We got lost on the way to the airport*). The papers are passed to the person on the left (it helps if the class is seated in a circle), and another line is added (e.g. *We missed our flight*). The story chains continue right round the class. Afterwards you can discuss if any of the problems were covered in the terms and conditions.

⚷
2 Possible answers
A Why don't you think about it and let us know in a day or so? Take your time. / Let me give you our phone number and email address. You can contact us when you've decided.
B I think this holiday would really suit you. / This is a very popular holiday, so it might sell out. / Would you like to confirm the booking now?

Reading
The small print

- Ask students to predict what they would expect to find in the terms and conditions on a holiday booking. Try to elicit the seven headings in **1**. Students work on their own for activities **1** and **2**, and check in pairs.

- Introduce **3** by telling a story of your own (invent if necessary).

⚷
1 1 d 2 e 3 f 4 g 5 a 6 b 7 c
2 1 a,b,c,g 2 d,e,f 3 a,b,c,d,e,f 4 g

Top margin

- Ask students if they have any credit or debit cards, and what method of payment they use to pay for things. Why do they use different methods?

Language spot
'If'

- Students may already be familiar with the First Conditional, but point out the use of modals (*may, must*, etc.) and the imperative as well as *will* in the 'result' clause, as these forms are probably more common in tourism.

- Let students do **1** and **2** in pairs and then report back. Do **3** in small groups. Award a prize for the most imaginative sentences.

⚷
1 2 future   4 will, must, may, imperative
    3 Present Simple
2 1 e 2 a 3 c 4 f 5 b 6 d

Pronunciation

- 🎧 Let students work in pairs and consult each other during **1**. Play the recording again if necessary. Encourage students to offer 'rules' about the spelling patterns in **2** and **3**. Ask students to look for more words that fit these patterns.

1 hat – standard, happen, cancel, cannot
pay – same, may, pay, take
sit – finish, if, will, written
five – price, right, flight, higher
2 The letter 'a' is pronounced /æ/ when followed by a single, final consonant or by two consonants. It is pronounced /eɪ/ when followed by 'y'. It is pronounced /eɪ/ when followed by a final, silent 'e'.
3 The letter 'i' is normally pronounced /i/. It is pronounced /aɪ/ when followed by silent 'e' or by 'gh'.

Speaking
Explaining booking conditions

- Get students to role-play all parts of the conversation, including welcoming, sitting down, explaining why they are here, etc.

It's my job

- Ask students what they know about tourism in China. Allow them time to answer the questions, and find out anything else that interests them.

Listening
Handing over tickets

- 🎧 Spend time looking at the ticket. Ask questions to check that they are reading the information correctly. For **2**, concentrate on the gist question. For **4**, the students listen intensively. Students compare answers in pairs between listenings.

O─⊓
1 1 Giorgio Bordoni   4 Toronto   6 out:depart 23.35; arrive 12.10
   2 12 August   5 Buenos Aires   return:depart 16.55; arrive 06.35
   3 AC 094   7 C$ 3,950.74
2 all of them except 1
3 Did he get it cheaper? Does it include taxes? Is it refundable?
4 1 details   4 Departing   7 Arrive   10 surcharges   13 up
   2 return   5 getting into 8 cost   11 refundable   14 to
   3 flight   6 Depart   9 fees   12 pay   15 bill

Speaking
Checking the details

- In **1**, monitor to check students have filled everything in, and then get them to exchange with a partner and do **2–4**.

Checklist, Key words, Next stop

- See suggestions on p.5. Remind students about transferring vocabulary into their Personal Learning Dictionaries.

➕ Additional activity

(stronger students)
China is one of the fastest growing tourism destinations and sources of tourism. Discuss what the impact of that has been on the tourism industry in general. Encourage students to research China on the Internet as a tourist destination and as a country that generates tourism.

➕ Additional activity

(all levels)
Run the activity as a mingling activity by randomly distributing the tickets at the start so that students first have to find their passenger (*Excuse me, are you the gentleman who's going to Jamaica?*). The students should not use their own names on the tickets. Doing the activity this way will allow students to practise polite introductory language as well as the target language of checking details.

12 Airport departures

Background

Modern airports are like 'mini-cities', so they must offer users all the facilities and services that this involves. Moreover, airports do not only provide services to travellers. They also serve the people and companies that use the airport professionally, such as aircraft crew, check-in staff, baggage handlers, and so on.

The turn-around team that Ali is a member of (*Listening* p.102) is a very good example of the type of key airport worker that passengers do not normally meet.

Of course, passengers are the central focus of an airport's activity, and in order to meet their needs, an airport must

- have good access by road and adequate parking
- have good alternative access by public transport
- have spacious areas for check-in, baggage handling, etc.
- offer food and other services
- maintain very high levels of security.

One indication of the status of the passenger in airport operations and air travel in general are air passengers' rights documents. The document on p.104–105 is from the European Union. This document was made public in February 2005, and covers four basic situations:

- Denied boarding – usually because of overbooking. Overbooking is common practice. It involves deliberately selling more tickets than there are seats on the aircraft. Airlines do this because on many flights there are always passengers who do not show up at the airport.
- Cancellation
- Long delays – the exact interpretation of 'long' depends on the type of flight, as the EU document explains
- Lost or damaged baggage.

The United States also has legislation regarding passengers' rights, but there is no single, easily available document as is the case with the EU, and in general compensation is not as clearly stipulated as in the EU. Airlines in the US are not required to give compensation for flights that are delayed or cancelled, for example.

Take off

- In small groups, students do **1** and **2**, and then report back to class. **3** can be done in open class.

✚ Additional activity

(all levels)
Use the plan of the airport to give directions from the check-in desk to various places. Students can do this in pairs and 'test' each other by seeing if they arrive at the correct place.
Note: the language of directions is not presented in this unit (it occurs in Book 2).

Where in the world?

- Allow students time to explore the plan of the airport.

> **⚓**
> **1** departures level
> **2** Departure: 1 h, 2 c/a, 3 a/c, 4 e, 5 i, 6 b   Arrival: 7 j, 8 d, 9 g, 10 k, 11 f

Vocabulary
Airport facilities and services

- Students do **1** without looking at the list. Do **2** and **3** in pairs and report back. **4** is a short creative exercise. Students can vote on the best designs.

> **⚓**
>
> | **2** | a 12 | b 1 | c 14 | d 9 | e 7 |
> |---|---|---|---|---|---|
>
> | **3** | 1 t | 5 a | 9 u | 13 v | 17 n |
> |---|---|---|---|---|---|
> | | 2 m | 6 o | 10 i | 14 y | 18 q |
> | | 3 p | 7 j | 11 w | 15 d | 19 e |
> | | 4 x | 8 b | 12 f | 16 l | 20 h |
>
> **4** luggage trolleys, email and Internet, smoking area, lifts, bar

➕ Additional activity

(all levels)

Get students to design their own personalized airport by getting them each to think of three activities they like doing when they have about two hours spare time (anywhere, not necessarily in an airport). In groups they pool the activities and decide which of them can be catered for in an airport of the future. They can design the airport layout and facilities (including symbols), and also discuss the staffing that would be necessary.

➕ Additional activity

(all levels)

Try to find an English-speaking tourism professional in the local area who could be interviewed, either face-to-face or via email. The questions in **2** can be used as a template for the interview.

➕ Additional activity

(stronger students)

Choose one of the facilities and do an in-depth study and prepare a special report (e.g. Business Services at Brussels Airport).

✱ Tip

check v control

These words are often confused, so it is worth checking students understand the difference. To check something is to make certain it is correct, to control something is to direct and manage something. The confusion is not helped by the fact that at Passport control, your passport is checked.

➕ Additional activity

(all levels)

Get students to say what the answers to the questions in **2** might be. This is developed in the next section.

Reading
Working in airports

● Set a time limit of one minute for **1**. Write answers on the board. Students read the article and find any jobs that they didn't think of before, and do **2**.

> **2** 1 d 2 a 3 e 4 b 5 c

Listening
An airport worker

● 🎧 Students read through **1** before listening, then compare answers in pairs before listening again. If necessary, pause the recording after each question in **2**, to allow time to write the answers.

> **1** 1 They meet the aircraft when they come in, service them, and get them ready for the outgoing flight.
> 2 about 12
> 3 Engineering degree, Aircraft Maintenance Engineers' licence
> 4 They have to get the jobs done in a minimum time.
> 5 sense of completion, being part of a team, working to a deadline
> 6 noise pollution, the dirt, oil, grease
> 7 free air travel
> 8 Take more engineering qualifications, and become a certified engineer.
>
> **2** 1 your job involve?   5 like most about your job?
> 2 people work in the team?   6 least?
> 3 do you have?   7 happy in your job?
> 4 a stressful job?   8 have any plans for the future?

Find out

● Visit the website of the local airport, and / or arrange an actual visit.

Vocabulary
Airport language

● Use the pictures to establish the three areas of the airport that are being looked at, before doing **1**. When going over the answers to **2**, check for accurate pronunciation, especially *aisle, suitcase, baggage*.

> **1** Information officer, check-in clerk, immigration officer
> **2** 1 ticket, passport (Passport control)   8 help (Information)
> 2 landed (Information)   9 baggage (Check-in)
> 3 suitcase (Check-in)   10 window (Check-in)
> 4 meeting (Information)   11 meeting point (Information)
> 5 purpose (Passport control)   12 board (Information)
> 6 sharp objects (Check-in)   13 checking in (Check-in)
> 7 help (Information)   14 aisle (Check-in)
> **3** 2, 7, 10, 11, 12

* Tip
Statistics from the Internet
Get students to find out the latest up-to-date statistics on the world's busiest airports by using a search engine. Let them decide which key words to type in. Report back to find out who has the latest figures.

Top margin

● Ask students to guess where the busiest passenger airports are. Refer to the list and ask if there are any surprises. Also ask if students have been to any of the airports. What did they think of them?

Language spot
Responding politely to questions and requests

● Students work through the activities in pairs and report back. At **3** and **5**, you can encourage students to continue the dialogues.

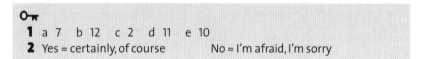

> **1** a 7 b 12 c 2 d 11 e 10
> **2** Yes = certainly, of course   No = I'm afraid, I'm sorry

Listening
Two airport dialogues

● ⌖ Students listen for the answers to **1** in the first listening. They can try to complete some of the gaps before they listen again for **2**.

> **1** 1 A: Information desk, B: Check-in
>   2 A: UA19 Atlanta, Gate G; B: Gate 23
> **2** A 1 help me   B 1 ticket
>   2 Certainly   2 checking in
>   3 UA 19   3 hand luggage
>   4 Atlanta   4 scales
>   5 it has   5 pack it
>   6 status   6 interfered with
>   7 Gate G   7 sharp objects
>   8 Gate G   8 you tell me
>   9 Gate G   9 I'm afraid
>   10 meeting point   10 boarding pass
>   11 you tell me   11 Gate 23
>   12 Yes, of course   12 nice flight
>   13 You're welcome

* Tip
Background noise
In an activity like this, do not worry if the students are close together and have trouble listening to each other. Developing speaking and listening skills in noisy environments is a useful thing to be able to do in tourism situations.

Speaking
The check-in and information desks

● Get students to read through the information files carefully first.

⊞ **Additional activity**
(all levels)
If you want to do some overt grammar work, you can work on modals (particularly *may* and *must*) and also revise the conditionals work from Unit 11.

⊞ **Additional activity**
(all levels)
Students choose one of the incidents, and prepare an email to their boss explaining what happened (see Writing bank 4 for a model).

⊞ **Additional activity**
(all levels)
Get students to think of other care / control, safety / security situations in other areas of tourism provision – e.g. in hotels, on other forms of transport.

Reading
Air passenger rights

● Use the open discussion / scene-setting stages in **1** and **2** to elicit and pre-teach important vocabulary. For **3**, make sure each group only focusses on their section of the text. For **4**, pair up students from each group and get them to explain what they have discovered.

Speaking
Incident and action log

● Working in small groups, get students to read through the six incidents, and, without looking at the other columns or referring back to the leaflet, decide what they would do. Then look at column 2 and see if the passengers did the same. When discussing the airline action in their groups, make sure students locate the exact part of the leaflet that gives the information.

> O━
> **Possible answers**
> 1 No, passengers should have been given €250 compensation as well as alternative flight, meals, and refreshments.
> 2 No, compensation should have been €600 as there was no advance warning.
> 3 OK. As the delay was under two hours, they didn't need to give the drink – but it was a nice gesture.
> 4 As the delay was over five hours, the two passengers who wanted to cancel should have been refunded.
> 5 OK. They didn't need to give the 10% discount voucher, but it was a nice gesture.
> 6 The airline didn't need to compensate because the written claim was received more than seven days after the incident. However, it was probably sensible as it was only one day late.

Customer care
Care or control?

● Keep the discussion fairly free and open.

Listening
Two more airport dialogues

● 🎧 Discuss **1** in open class. Students compare answers to **2** in pairs before reporting back. They can try to complete the sentences in **3** before they listen again. Point out that there may be more than one word per gap.

> O━
> **2** 1 A = care, B = control
>   2 A: Passenger on flight AZ402 has not received suitcase. It's not at oversized baggage desk.
>   B: Passengers arrive late for flight and cabin doors have been shut. Passenger gets angry and tries to go through. Official threatens to call security.
>   3 A: Official fills in a form to trace suitcase and puts message through to arrivals where passenger's sister is waiting.
>   B: Official refers them to airline desk to book next available flight.

3 1 Go over, by mistake
2 understand
3 can you start to
4 just, we'll sort
5 sorry, can't go
6 you're too late
7 do not go through, I'll have to
8 if you see, she'll make sure

✳ Tip

Form and function

It is important for students to be aware that different *forms* (grammar structures) can be used to achieve the same *function* (e.g. giving an order), and that selecting the appropriate form, as well as the right intonation and body language, are very important in tourism.

Language spot

Giving orders and stopping people doing something

- Use the symbols to identify the situations in **1**. Point out that different forms can often be used to achieve a different style or 'register' (e.g. politeness, firmness, formality / informality), but that intonation and general manner / body language are also just as important. Students work in pairs on **3** and **4**, then compare answers in open class.

⊶

2 Possible answers

As pointed out above, a lot depends on intonation and body language, but the first two are more direct.

3 1 Go over to the oversized baggage desk.
Sir, do not go through the barrier!
2 Can you start to fill in this form, so we can trace it?
3 I'm sorry, but you can't go through there.
I'm afraid you're too late.
I'm afraid that's not possible.
4 If you just wait over there, we'll sort this out.
If you do, I'll have to call security.
If you see my colleague at the airline desk over there, she'll make sure that you get on the next available flight.

Pronunciation

- 🎧 These activities attempt to raise students' awareness of the impact of the wrong tone of voice, and to give them practice in finding the appropriate tone. In **1**, encourage students to consult with partners as they listen. In **3**, it is very important to get students to imagine themselves in the role of the airport official.

Speaking

Controlling passengers

- Students do **1** individually, then do **2** in pairs.

Checklist, Key words, Next stop

- See suggestions on p.5. Remind students about transferring vocabulary into their Personal Learning Dictionaries.

➕ Additional activity

(all levels)

If you want, you can end the unit with a large-scale airport simulation. Set up check-in desks, information desks, passport / security control, and departure gates. Divide the class into two groups: airport staff (distributed at the various locations) and passengers (each of whom can be given a particular 'emotion card' – e.g. nervous, excited, impatient, etc). There may be a sense of chaos, not unlike a real airport at busy times.

You can add a further dimension to the activity by appointing two students as a TV crew filming 'a day at the airport' and interviewing staff and officials (use a real video camera if possible). This will have the added advantage of 'mopping up' spare students who are not in the action at various points. Watch the resulting film for language work – and for fun.

Instructions for communication activities

Unit 1

1 Description bingo

1 Put students in groups of three or four, so that each player has a different bingo card.

2 Make sure they understand the words on their card.

3 Shuffle the job cards and place them face down, in a pile.

4 The first player takes the top job card and must give sentences about the job on the card, without saying the word.

EXAMPLES

He / she works in / at a _____ (place).

He / she works in the _____ (industry sector).

He / she _____ (a skill or routine)

5 The other players guess the word, the first player giving extra sentences if necessary.

6 When the group has guessed the word correctly, those players who have the word on their bingo card cross it out.

7 The second player then takes the next individual card and gives a definition, and so on.

8 The first player to cross out all his or her words is the winner.

2 Who am I?

1 Get students to take one of the job cards and without looking at it, stick it or clip it to their back (another student can help).

2 The students then go round the class asking each other a 'yes / no' question (one question per student) and answering similar questions until they know who they are – for example, *Do I work at the airport? Do I have to be willing to work long hours?*

3 If they finish early, they can take another card and repeat the exercise until everyone has found out their first job.

3 Grouping and ranking

1 Put students in pairs or small groups and give each group a set of the job cards.

2 The students arrange the cards into groups (or rank them in an order), without making the grouping too obvious (for example, not simply the place where they work).

3 The other students then have to guess how the cards have been grouped or ranked.

4 Odd one out

1 Put the students in groups. They take turns to choose four of the job cards, one of which should be an 'odd one out', e.g. *waiter, pilot, flight attendant, ski instructor* (*pilot* is the odd one out because he or she does not usually talk face to face with tourists – but there could be other reasons!).

2 The other students have to guess which one is the odd one out and why.

Unit 5

1 Put students in groups of three or four. Tell them that they have to arrange the posters and display sections for the window of a travel agency. There are twelve possibilities, but unfortunately there is only room for eight posters in the window.

2 The students must decide which eight they are going to use and how they will arrange them (they are all the same size and they must be in two rows of four).

3 When they have made their final decision, the students go round and visit the other windows, asking why they decided on their arrangement.

Unit 7

[Note: for classes with more than twelve students, the roles can be doubled up – i.e. two people on a hotel information desk, and visitors in couples.]

1 Divide the class in half.

2 Put the As behind desks (if possible), and give each person the information on a different hotel in New York. They should try to 'sell' their hotel and make it fit the needs of the visitors.

3 Give Bs one of the 'requirement cards' for potential visitors. Bs should visit each of the Hotel Information Desks and find the hotel that is most suitable to their requirements. Make sure they visit all the hotels so they have a wide choice.

4 Get students to report back on their final choices.

Unit 8

1 Divide into groups. Give each group three different tourism products or services from the cards. The students will have to sell them to students from other groups in the market place of the classroom.

2 In their groups, students decide (a) the strengths and weaknesses of each of the items (they can do a SWOT analysis), and (b) how they are going to sell each of the items.

3 The class mingle and, working as individuals, try

to sell their products. They can sell the same product to different people. In each encounter they must buy one thing and sell another. Get them to make a note of the items they sell and buy.

4 When they have spoken to as many people as possible, students get back into their original groups and discuss the most popular items.

Unit 9

Make or copy enough sets of the cards. For game 1 you will need one set for each group of students. For game 2 you will need one set for every four students. For game 3 you will only need one set for the whole class.

There are 24 cards. There are three 'suits' (airline code, airport code, and famous city).

1 Happy families

1 Students work in groups of three or four. Deal out all the cards. Make sure that each player has at least five cards.

2 The aim of the game is to collect full sets (i.e. airline / airport / city from the same country), by 'swapping' with other students. They mustn't show their cards to each other. Instead they should ask questions like:
Have you got the airport code for Spain?
Would you like New York?

2 Eliciting bridge

1 Put students in groups of four, with two pairs working as partners and sitting opposite each other.

2 The cards should be face down in the middle of the table.

3 Students take turns to take a card from the top of the pile. They have to elicit the contents of the card from their partner, for example:
If it is a code, they should say, *What is the airline / airport code for Alitalia / Rome?*
If it is a famous city, they should say, *Name a famous city in Italy.*
The partner is allowed three guesses. If they get it right, they win the point.

4 The winners are the pair with the most points after they have got to the end of the pile, or at the end of a time limit.

3 Have you ever?

[Note: as Present Perfect for experience is the language spot in Unit 10, it may be an idea to use the cards for game 3 after you've done Unit 10.]

1 Give three or four cards to each student.

2 Students stand up and mingle, using the information on the cards to ask each other questions such as:

Have you ever been to Toronto?
Have you ever been to Toronto airport?
Have you ever flown with Air Canada?

3 They get a point for every person who answers 'yes' to any of the questions – but they must ask them for details of their visit or trip.

Unit 10

1 Put students in groups of four and tell them that they are tour operators for the same company. They have one more tour to add to their programme for next year in which they want to target 18- to 35-year-olds. First, they should make a list of the things which that age group looks for in a holiday.

Example

the chance to meet and get to know other young people

2 Designate each student in the group A, B, C, or D and then re-group them by letter.

3 Give each group the tour card which corresponds to their letter (cards A, B, C, and D).

4 In their new groups, they discuss the reasons why theirs is a good choice (based on the things they listed in stage 1) and note them on their card.

5 When they have discussed the advantages of their particular tour in detail, they return to their original group, and argue for their tour to be included.

Unit 12

Ask the students to work in groups of three or four.

1 Students take turns to choose a seat number on the plane. There are four categories: A = Tourism vocabulary, B = Knowledge of tourism industry, C = Language spot, D = Your area. Each row corresponds to a unit of the book.

2 The student has to answer the question or perform the task. The rest of the group must decide if they have answered the question or performed the task well. If the group decides that they have, then they get the seat. The teacher will be the referee if necessary.

3 The winner is the person who has the most seats at the end.

1 Grammar test

1 Look at the job advertisement. Complete these statements made by someone who does the job. Use the correct form of one of the verbs in the list and the word or phrase in brackets.

speak   use   wear   work

EXAMPLE I have to enjoy *working with people*. (people)

1 I have to _____ (uniform)
2 I have to be able _____ (as part of a team)
3 I have to be good at _____ (on the telephone)
4 I have to know how _____ (a computer)
5 I have to be willing _____ (long hours)
6 Sometimes I have to _____ (night shift)
7 Occasionally I _____ (hotel on the beach)

2 For sentences 2, 3, 4, and 5, write the questions that the job interviewer might ask.

EXAMPLE *Do you enjoy working with people?*

2 _____
3 _____
4 _____
5 _____

3 For sentences 1, 6, and 7, write the question that a colleague or friend might ask to find out about the job.

1 Do you _____ ?
6 How often _____ ?
7 How often _____ ?

4 Ruth works as a check-in clerk at a busy airport, but this week is her week off. Look at her normal work routine and what she is doing this week. Make sentences like the example.

Routine	Work	This week
Get up	7 a.m. (always)	10 a.m.
Morning	Work at airport check-in desk (usually)	Go to gym
Lunch	In staff canteen (usually)	With friends or family
Afternoon	Work in departure lounge (sometimes)	Shopping
Evening	Watch TV (usually)	Out with friends
Go to bed	10 p.m. (always)	Midnight

EXAMPLE
When I work, I always get up at 7 a.m., but this week I'm getting up at 10 a.m.

1 In the morning, _____
2 _____
3 _____
4 _____
5 _____

Vacancy at the Hotel Civica

The Hotel Civica has the following vacancy:

Hotel receptionist

- Must be friendly and smart (uniform supplied)
- Ability to work as part of a team
- Good telephone manner
- Knowledge of computers essential
- Long hours (0800 to 1800) six days a week
- Work nights one week in four
- Occasional work at our other hotel on the beach

1 Communication

i Go to p.66 for instructions

Job cards

PILOT	RECEPTIONIST	HOTEL MANAGER	BAGGAGE HANDLER
TOUR GUIDE	WAITER	AIRLINE CHECK-IN CLERK	HOTEL NIGHT MANAGER
FLIGHT ATTENDANT	RESORT REP	CLEANER	TICKET COLLECTOR
TOURIST INFORMATION OFFICER	CHEF	CAR RENTAL SUPERVISOR	SKI INSTRUCTOR
TRAVEL AGENT	PORTER	TOUR OPERATOR	CHILDREN'S ACTIVITY ORGANIZER

Bingo cards

Student A

HOTEL NIGHT MANAGER	CLEANER
TOUR GUIDE	TOUR OPERATOR
TOURIST INFORMATION OFFICER	RESORT REP
RECEPTIONIST	CAR RENTAL SUPERVISOR

Student C

WAITER	CHILDREN'S ACTIVITY ORGANIZER
RESORT REP	BAGGAGE HANDLER
TOURIST INFORMATION OFFICER	PORTER
AIRLINE CHECK-IN CLERK	CAR RENTAL SUPERVISOR

Student B

HOTEL MANAGER	SKI INSTRUCTOR
FLIGHT ATTENDANT	TOUR GUIDE
CHEF	BAGGAGE HANDLER
TOUR OPERATOR	PORTER

Student D

TICKET COLLECTOR	CHILDREN'S ACTIVITY ORGANIZER
HOTEL NIGHT MANAGER	PILOT
FLIGHT ATTENDANT	RECEPTIONIST
HOTEL MANAGER	CLEANER

2 Grammar test

1 Complete the description of Canada with *are*, *is*, *has got*, or nothing.

Canada

Canada _____ [1] the world's second largest country. It _____ [2] located to the north of the USA and _____ [3] stretches across six time zones. Canada _____ [4] a population of approximately 32 million that _____ [5] consists of many different nationalities: there _____ [6] an English-speaking majority but there _____ [7] also a large French-speaking minority in Quebec.

The climate _____ [8] varied: the north _____ [9] a polar climate, but on the Pacific coast around Vancouver there _____ [10] warm winters, where temperatures rarely fall below zero. There _____ [11] many attractions for tourists. Canada _____ [12] some of the most spectacular scenery in the world. There _____ [13] mountains, great plains, and many rivers, along which most of the big cities _____ [14] located. There _____ [15] lots of things for the twenty million visitors a year who come to Canada to do.

2 Write questions for the FAQ section of a website about Canada.

1 Where / located? _____
2 What / population? _____
3 What / climate / like? _____
4 What / attractions? _____
5 Where / cities? _____
6 How many / visitors every year? _____

3 Correct the mistakes in this postcard from a tour rep writing to her friend. (There are eleven mistakes.)

Hi Julie

Well, here I am in Australia. We stay in Sydney at the moment, which located in the south-east. It's just great! There is so many things to do. It got night-clubs, restaurants, and there is some fascinating tourist attractions. I took a group to the Sydney Harbour Bridge today, which is fantastic, because you can enjoying some great views. I've got a great group – they are enjoying the trip, and I think they are liking me as well. Tomorrow we're flying to Alice Springs and then to Ayers Rock, which is lying in the centre of Australia. The weather are very hot there. You can to do so much in this wonderful country. Our brochure is right: Australia offer everything under the sun!

Bye

Angela

2 Communication

A

1 Tell your partner about maximum temperatures in the Balearic Islands.

2 Ask your partner about maximum temperatures in Sydney so that you can complete your temperature graph.

3 Repeat the activity for rainfall.

Balearic Islands

Month	Max temp (°C)	Average rainfall (mm)
Jan	14	48
Feb	15	39
Mar	17	39
Apr	19	45
May	22	34
Jun	26	20
Jul	29	9
Aug	29	24
Sep	27	54
Oct	23	86
Nov	18	62
Dec	15	57

Sydney

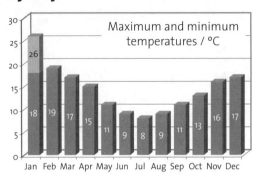

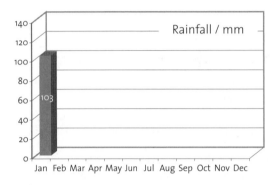

B

1 Ask your partner about maximum temperatures in the Balearic Islands, so that you can complete your temperature graph.

2 Tell your partner about maximum temperatures in Sydney.

3 Repeat the activity for rainfall.

Sydney

Month	Max temp (°C)	Average rainfall (mm)
Jan	26	103
Feb	26	113
Mar	25	134
Apr	22	126
May	19	121
Jun	17	131
Jul	16	101
Aug	18	81
Sep	20	69
Oct	22	79
Nov	24	83
Dec	25	78

Balearic Islands

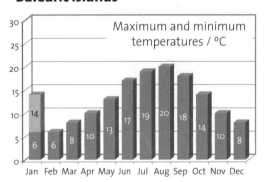

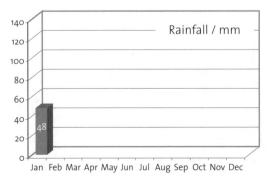

3 Grammar test

1 Look at these answers given by a tour operator at a trade fair. What questions did the travel agent ask?

1 _____

We specialize in adventure travel.

2 _____

We offer a wide variety of tours from mountain biking to scuba diving.

3 _____

No, they're available to any age group – but the tourists need to be fit.

4 _____

It's a package tour, so everything is included.

5 _____

We use local hotels, usually three-star.

6 _____

Standard commission is 15%, but we can negotiate depending on volume of sales.

2 Which preposition goes with which time phrase: *at, for, in, on,* or nothing?

Saturday	6 a.m.	Christmas	the weekend	today
10 o'clock	next week	2008	the winter	the evening
breakfast	this afternoon	a long time	two weeks	three years
14 August	a year's time	yesterday	my birthday	13:00

3 Correct the mistakes in this email from a travel agent to the tour operator arranging the 'Glimpse of the Baltics' tour.

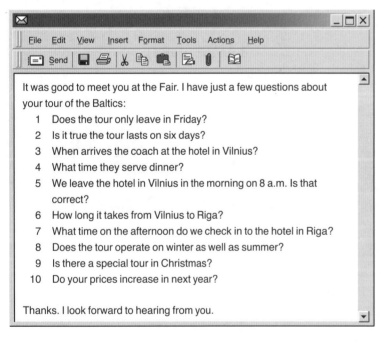

It was good to meet you at the Fair. I have just a few questions about your tour of the Baltics:

1 Does the tour only leave in Friday?
2 Is it true the tour lasts on six days?
3 When arrives the coach at the hotel in Vilnius?
4 What time they serve dinner?
5 We leave the hotel in Vilnius in the morning on 8 a.m. Is that correct?
6 How long it takes from Vilnius to Riga?
7 What time on the afternoon do we check in to the hotel in Riga?
8 Does the tour operate on winter as well as summer?
9 Is there a special tour in Christmas?
10 Do your prices increase in next year?

Thanks. I look forward to hearing from you.

3 Communication

Group A Tour Operators

You are at a trade fair to sell your new tours to travel agents.

Add a third tour to the chart. Be prepared to answer questions about tours from the travel agents.

	Tour 1	Tour 2	Tour 3
Location	Nepal, Himalayas	River Nile, Egypt	
Activities	Trekking	Sightseeing, visiting pyramids, etc.	
Length	Three weeks	Ten days	
Accommodation	Lodges and campsites	Hotels and on-board cruise ship	
Transport	Flights to Nepal, jeep, and walking	Flights to Egypt, cruise ship on Nile	
Price category $ to $$$$$	$$	$$$	
Group discount	Not available	One free place for groups of eight	
Commission payable	15%	20%	

At the end, compare the tours you sold.

- -

Group B Travel Agents

You are meeting at a trade fair in order to plan your programmes for next year. You are looking for one more tour to add to your programme. Visit the tour operators and ask about their tours.

You also want to get high commissions if possible.

As you talk to the Tour Operators, complete this chart. Before you start, think about the questions you will ask.

EXAMPLES
What's the location of your tour?   *How long is the tour?*
What activities do the tourists take part in?   *Is there a commission payable?*

Location				
Activities				
Length				
Accommodation				
Transport				
Price category $ to $$$$$				
Group discount				
Commission payable				

At the end, compare the tours you chose.

4 Grammar test

1 Match the questions in A with the answers in B, and then choose the correct word or phrase for the start of the answer.

A		Because / Because of / To / For / In case	B	
1	Why do I need a visa?		a	it's full.
2	Why can't I smoke on the plane?		b	there's an emergency.
3	Why must I open my suitcase?		c	pleasure.
4	Why should I listen to the safety announcement?		d	get into the country.
5	Why is check-in taking so long?		e	a staff shortage.
6	Why can't I get on the flight?		f	it's not allowed.
7	Why do you want to see my boarding card?		g	a delay in loading the baggage.
8	Why are you travelling to Brussels?		h	you get lost and need to phone me.
9	Why do I need the phone number of the hotel?		i	a security check.
10	Why is the flight late?		j	check you're in the right seat.

Which question is not asked by a traveller?

2

1   Complete the sentences with the correct tense of the verb in A.

	A	B
1 The graph shows that the number of international arrivals _____ since 1950.	rise	dramatic
2 From 1950 to 1960 the number of international tourist arrivals _____ from 30 million to 80 million.	grow	steady
3 Between 1950 and 2000 the figure _____ by nearly 28-fold.	increase	sharp
4 In the present day the number of arrivals _____ to grow _____ .	continue	dramatic
5 By 2020 the figure _____ 1580 million.	be	–

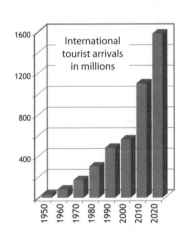

International tourist arrivals in millions

2   What are the adverb forms of the adjectives in B? Insert them in the sentences.

4 Communication

1 You are taking two trips in the next year. Complete the details in the chart. On each trip you are taking an unusual object. You can choose from the pictures, or think of your own if you prefer.

	Where from?	Destination	Purpose	Length of stay	Unusual object
1	Your home town	New York	Shopping and sightseeing	One week	
2				Three weeks	

2 Walk around and ask all the other students in the class about their trips, the purpose, and the unusual item. Make notes.

Name	Where from?	Destination	Purpose	Length of stay	Unusual object (and reason)

3 When you have finished compare with other students to see if you have the same answers.

● Who had the most interesting journey?

● Who had the most unusual object?

5 Grammar test

1 Write the questions on this Initial Enquiry Form. Make sure they agree with the answers that are given. Some of the questions are 'open' and some are 'closed'.

Initial Enquiry Form

	Question	Answer
Name	What's your name?	John Terry
Contact no.	1	0796 1313126
Booked with us before	2	Yes, last year ... to Cyprus.
Destination	3	No, we wanted to try somewhere different.
Type of holiday	4	Beach, relaxation.
Dates	5	Yes, we do. From 17 or 18 June.
Length of stay	6	For two weeks.
Size of party	7	Just the two of us.
Accommodation type	8	Just a simple hotel near the beach.

2 Look at what five customers in a travel agency say. Match their wishes and interests with a holiday, and give advice starting with the words given.

1 'My husband and I are looking for somewhere quiet and romantic – but not too expensive – to celebrate our first wedding anniversary. Any ideas?'

    Why _____
    _____
    _____

2 'We've got three young children, so we want somewhere where there's plenty for them to do, and space to play. We like cycling. What can you suggest?'

    How _____
    _____
    _____

3 'A group of us are going to university after the summer. We want to go away for a few weeks, see a bit of culture, have a good time, but not spend too much. Any ideas?'

    If _____
    _____
    _____

4 'Our company has had a very successful year, so we want to celebrate in style. What do you think?'

    Have _____
    _____
    _____

5 'We want to go somewhere different – outdoors, exciting, seeing new cultures. What have you got?'

    Your _____
    _____
    _____

Choose from these holidays.

- a beach holiday in the Caribbean
- a weekend break in Prague
- an adventure holiday trekking in the Himalayas
- a one month 'Inter-rail' holiday travelling around Europe by train
- a weekend in a five-star hotel in New York
- a week in a farmhouse in the French countryside
- a ten-day Mediterranean cruise
- a day trip to Disneyland Paris

5 Communication

i Go to p.66 for instructions

Next year, why not try...

... a luxury cruise in the Caribbean?

DISCOVER SOUTH AFRICA

BUY	SELL
$ 1.00	€ 0.79
$ 1.00	¥ 114.1
$ 1.00	£ 0.55
£ 1.00	€ 1.43
£ 1.00	¥ 206
£ 1.00	F 2.26

Travel and Tours is a member of the National Association of Travel Agencies

NATA

2 weeks,
Lanzarote,
self-catering, £ 230

1 week **Malta,**
half-board £ 190

2 weeks
Brittany,
campsite, £ 140

Late adventure deals:

trekking in Nepal,

diving in the Maldives,

adventure sports in New Zealand

-ask inside for details

We offer:

- Advice on visa and passport applications
- Coach tours and trips
- Foreign currency and traveller's cheques
- Hotel bookings
- Package holidays
- Train tickets
- Transport information
- Travel insurance

EUROPE

Manager
Sarah Bowles

Assistant Manager
Graham Harrison

Sales team

Frances
Smith

Helen
Farell

Chris
Gilligan

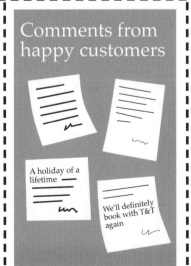

Comments from happy customers

A holiday of a lifetime

We'll definitely book with T&T again

TRAVEL & TOURS
the pleasure is yours

6 Grammar test

1 Complete this email from a travel agent to a customer, using the adjectives in brackets and adding any other words that may be necessary.

	Venice–Simplon Orient Express	Trans-Siberian Express
From / to	Paris to Istanbul	Moscow to Beijing
Time	6 days	8 days
Cost	$$$$	$$
Comfort	*****	***

2 Use the timetable to correct the false information given by a transport official.

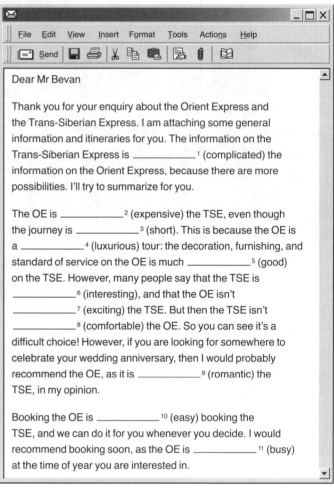

Golden Gate Ferry

Leave Sausalito	Arrive San Francisco
Monday to Friday	
7:10	7:40
10:10	10:40
1:10p	1:40p
4:10p	4:40p
7:10p	7:40p
Saturday and Sunday	
11:50	12:20
2:50p	3:20p
5:50p	6:20

Notes:

1 Discounts for seniors available
2 Bicycles allowed subject to space availability

Dear Mr Bevan

Thank you for your enquiry about the Orient Express and the Trans-Siberian Express. I am attaching some general information and itineraries for you. The information on the Trans-Siberian Express is _____ [1] (complicated) the information on the Orient Express, because there are more possibilities. I'll try to summarize for you.

The OE is _____ [2] (expensive) the TSE, even though the journey is _____ [3] (short). This is because the OE is a _____ [4] (luxurious) tour: the decoration, furnishing, and standard of service on the OE is much _____ [5] (good) on the TSE. However, many people say that the TSE is _____ [6] (interesting), and that the OE isn't _____ [7] (exciting) the TSE. But then the TSE isn't _____ [8] (comfortable) the OE. So you can see it's a difficult choice! However, if you are looking for somewhere to celebrate your wedding anniversary, then I would probably recommend the OE, as it is _____ [9] (romantic) the TSE, in my opinion.

Booking the OE is _____ [10] (easy) booking the TSE, and we can do it for you whenever you decide. I would recommend booking soon, as the OE is _____ [11] (busy) at the time of year you are interested in.

Passenger question	Transport official	Corrected information
Example: *When does the first ferry leave?*	*7:20*	*No, it doesn't. It leaves at 7:10.*
1 When does the first ferry arrive at SF?	7:45	
2 Is that seven days a week?	Yes	
3 How frequent are the ferries?	Every 2 hours	
4 What time does the last ferry leave?	8:10 pm	
5 Can I take my bicycle?	No	
6 Are there any discounts available?	No, there aren't.	

6 Communication

1 Name two types of transport that a tourist might use to get to the airport.

2 Talk about the last time you got a taxi.

3 Describe the different ways of getting from your house to the nearest airport.

4 Name three people who work at an airport.

8 Give the names of a train company, a coach company, and an airline from your country.

7 What's the most unusual type of transport you've ever taken?

6 Which do you prefer, travel by train or travel by coach? Why?

5 If you worked at an airport, which job would you least like, and why?

9 Without using the word, describe a type of transport for the other students to guess.

10 Name three types of water transport.

11 Which form of transport is best for city sightseeing? Why?

12 What are the opposites of these adjectives: *cheap, safe, comfortable?*

16 Give directions to a visitor to your city who wants to know about the best way to get around.

15 Name four facilities that passengers might find on a cruise ship.

14 Talk for 30 seconds about your favourite form of transport.

13 Do you know anyone who has travelled by helicopter? Talk about their journey.

17 Where can tourists rent bicycles in your town / city?

18 Name three journeys you can take using animals.

19 What types of transport are these cities famous for: San Francisco, Venice, Amsterdam, London?

20 Describe the exact journey (and transport types) you would take to get from where you are now to your favourite place in the world.

Instructions

You need a copy of the board, a coin, and a marker for each player.

In turn, toss a coin. Tails – move one square. Heads – move two squares.

If a player can't answer a question, they miss the next turn.

Players should not repeat the same answer that another player gave.

The winner is the first person to reach number 20.

7 Grammar test

1 Look at this plan of 'Camping Bretagne'. Complete the gaps with words and phrases from the box. Some may be needed more than once, some not at all.

behind	between	from	in	in front of	in the heart of
near	next to	on	opposite	under	within

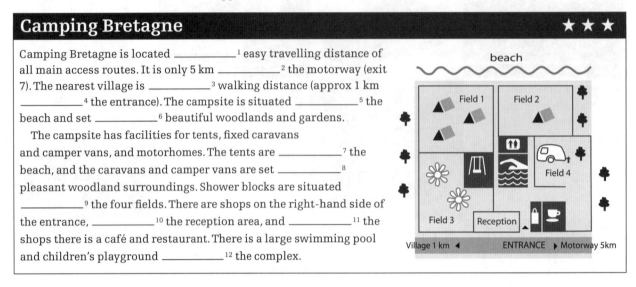

Camping Bretagne ★ ★ ★

Camping Bretagne is located _____[1] easy travelling distance of all main access routes. It is only 5 km _____[2] the motorway (exit 7). The nearest village is _____[3] walking distance (approx 1 km _____[4] the entrance). The campsite is situated _____[5] the beach and set _____[6] beautiful woodlands and gardens.

The campsite has facilities for tents, fixed caravans and camper vans, and motorhomes. The tents are _____[7] the beach, and the caravans and camper vans are set _____[8] pleasant woodland surroundings. Shower blocks are situated _____[9] the four fields. There are shops on the right-hand side of the entrance, _____[10] the reception area, and _____[11] the shops there is a café and restaurant. There is a large swimming pool and children's playground _____[12] the complex.

beach

Field 1 Field 2

Field 4

Field 3   Reception

Village 1 km ◀   ENTRANCE ▶ Motorway 5km

2 Complete these questions asked by the reservations clerk at a hotel.

1 What type _____? A double en-suite

2 When would _____? From 15 to 17 January

3 How _____? By credit card

4 What's _____? J P Garcia

5 How _____? G-A-R-C-I-A

6 What's _____? September 2010

3 The Hotel Metropolitan has been renovated. Look at the plan of the new hotel. Amend the description below, which comes from an old brochure.

Hotel Metropolitan ★ ★ ★ ★

As you enter the hotel you will find the Reception on your right. Behind the reception desk are administration offices. On the left-hand side as you enter there is a large office and next to it, a little further on, a smaller office. Just beyond this, after a small doorway that leads to the indoor and outdoor gardens and the car park, is another office. Opposite the main entrance are the lifts and stairs that will take you to the guest rooms. As you stand at the reception desk and look to your left, you will see the restaurant and behind, a little further down the corridor, is the bar.

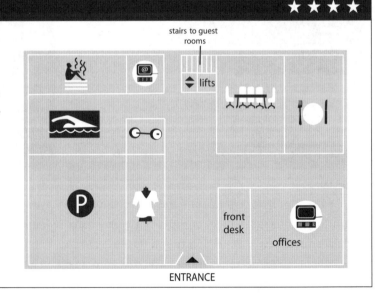

stairs to guest rooms

⇕ lifts

P

front desk

offices

ENTRANCE

7 Communication

i Go to p.66 for instructions

A

Holiday Inn Wall Street $ $ $ $

In the heart of the financial district, this is NY's most technologically advanced hotel. Designed for the business traveller.

St Regis New York $ $ $ $ $

One of NY's most luxurious hotels. Situated in the heart of the theater district, and decorated with fabulous carpets, paintings, and chandeliers.

Hotel Chelsea $ $ $

Hotel where many famous artists and musicians have stayed, from Bob Dylan to Sid Vicious. Decorated in an unusual and bohemian style.

Plaza Hotel $ $ $ $

Probably NY's most famous hotel in NY's most famous location – 5th Avenue. Featured in many Hollywood films. Great location for shopping.

Chelsea International Hostel $ $

Private rooms with basic facilities. Communal kitchens and TV lounges. Fashionable central location.

Coney Island Beach Resort $ $ $ $ $

Right on the beach, but close to the subway and access to downtown NY. Lots to do for all the family and good value.

B

Business person
- Near city center. Financial district if possible
- Luxury, in order to impress clients
- Price not a problem
- Would like a pool or sauna

Group of friends on a pre-Christmas shopping trip
- Near the shops and city center
- Also want to do some sightseeing
- Reasonable budget, but cheaper accommodation will mean more for shopping

Couple celebrating wedding anniversary
- Silver wedding (25 years) so want something a bit special
- Enjoy cultural events and dancing
- Price not too much of a problem if it's good quality

Family: mum, dad, and two children (aged 9 and 13)
- Want to see the famous sights, but would also like to have things for the kids to do
- Nothing too expensive

Group of three students
- Interested in music and the club scene, but would also like to get to the beach and do a bit of shopping
- Don't have much money

Company looking for a good hotel to send three of their best employees (and partners) as a reward for excellent service. (You decide what type of company.)
- Price not a big problem – they're worth it!

8 Grammar test

1 Choose the correct word or words to complete the memo from the Managing Director of a Tour Operator company to her staff.

> **Memo to staff:**
>
> As I am sure you are aware, this year's figures have been disappointing. Our campaigns, mainly *gear / geared / hope / hoped* [1] to the adult and senior markets, have not been successful. Next year we are *hope / hope to / hoping / hoping to* [2] increase business significantly. We are going to *gear / gearing / let / letting* [3] our marketing campaign *to / towards / –* [4] the youth market. I will *let / letting* [5] you know the details soon.
>
> I *gear / hope / let* [6] you can see the importance of this new direction. If you have any questions, please *gear / hope / let* [7] me know.
>
> Sandra Lukas
>
> MD

2 Change the adjective in brackets into a superlative and then complete the sentence for yourself.

1 The _____ (old) building I've visited is _____.

2 The _____ (cheap) hotel in my town is probably _____.

3 The _____ (new) hotel in my town is _____.

4 The _____ (beautiful) beach I've been to is _____.

5 The _____ (big) airport I've been to is _____.

6 The _____ (expensive) resort in my country is probably _____.

7 The _____ (small) room I've stayed in was in _____.

3 Change the adjectives in **2** to one of the alternatives in the box.

economical   luxurious   modern   gorgeous
historic   tiny   large

4 Correct the mistakes in these marketing slogans.

1 Let us to help you relax, Caribbean-style.

2 For one of the most exciting experiences of you life, come to China.

3 Book with e-line: nothing could be more easy.

4 Tom's taxis: we're geared meeting your needs.

5 Stay at the most luxury hotel on the Costa Brava.

6 Hire the Minimax – the bigest small car on the market.

8 Communication

i Go to p.66 for instructions

Inflatable pillow, mask, and comfort pack for air travel 	Portable waste disposal unit. Ideal for the 'green' tourist	Audio language course (you decide which language)
Mobile phone conversion kit, so you can phone internationally easily	A pair of binoculars 	Electronic translating machine 
International coach voucher, giving 100 km free travel on coaches in any country	Insurance service, in case you have cash or goods stolen or lost	Fast check-in pass to help you get through airports quickly
Two weeks' supply of the food or drink you will miss most when travelling	Currency converter. It calculates the exchange rate quickly	Personal security kit (whistle, defence spray, etc.) 

9 Grammar test

1 Anita Rauch is a flight attendant. Look at the list of things she likes and dislikes about her job. Write eight sentences.

EXAMPLE

I really love going to interesting cities.

1 _____
2 _____
3 _____
4 _____
5 _____
6 _____
7 _____
8 _____

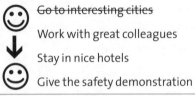

☺ ~~Go to interesting cities~~

Work with great colleagues

↓

Stay in nice hotels

☺ Give the safety demonstration

😐 Wear a uniform

☹ Serve food

Work on long-haul flights

↓

Spend time away from my boyfriend

☹ Deal with difficult passengers

2 Write the questions – direct and indirect – from the questionnaire prompts.

Questionnaire	Direct question	Indirect question
1 Age?	*How old are you?*	*Would you mind telling me how old you are?*
2 Travelling alone?	*Are you travelling alone?*	*Could you tell me if you are travelling alone?*
3 Occupation?		Can …
4 Destination?		Would …
5 Reason for journey?		Could …
6 Airline?		Can …
7 Length of flight?		Would …
8 First time with this airline?		Could …
9 Frequent flyer?		Can …
10 Like flying in general?		Would …
11 Join our Frequent Flyer Programme?		Could …
12 Give me your email address?		Can …

3 Match the advice about conducting questionnaires in A to the statements and questions in B.

A	B
1 Be polite when you get the person's attention.	a Many thanks for giving me your time.
2 Say what the questionnaire is about.	b Really? That's interesting.
3 Ask permission before you ask any questions.	c This will only take five minutes.
4 Tell the person how long the interview will last.	d Excuse me, madam. I wonder if I could trouble you for a moment?
5 Be interested in what the person is saying.	e I'm doing a survey about air travel.
6 Thank the person at the end.	f Would you mind if I asked you some questions?

9 Communication

i Go to p.67 for instructions

AIRLINE	AIRPORT	FAMOUS CITY
BA	LHR	London
IB	MAD	Madrid
AF	ORY	Paris
AZ	ROM	Rome
AA	NYC	New York
CA	YTO	Toronto
QF	SYD	Sydney
ANZ	AKL	Auckland

10 Grammar test

1 Read this background information on a tour company. Put the verbs in the correct tense, Present Perfect or Past Simple. See the example.

2 Write the dialogue using the prompts given.

A ever / water-skiing?

B no

A ever / windsurfing?

B yes

A when?

B last year

A where?

B Greece

A like it?

B yes

Access Abroad

Access Abroad _was_ (be) originally called Tour-ability. It
_____ [1] (start) in 1970, and _____ [2] (be) one of
the first companies in the UK to specialize in tour packages
for groups with disabilities. Since those early days the
company _____ [3] (grow). Originally tours only
_____ [4] (go) to Switzerland, but now Access Abroad
arranges tours throughout the world. Recent tours
_____ [5] (include) trips to France, Belgium, Canada,
Spain, and the Czech Republic.

_Client comment: 'I go every year with Access Abroad,
and I _____ [6] (have) some amazing experiences.
Last year I _____ [7] (visit) Canada and Spain.
Next year? Who knows where!'_

3 Choose the correct word to complete this description of a special holiday.

A gastronomic week in France

1 The week _is / are_ organized by one of France's leading tour operators.

2 This region of France _boasts / presents_ some of the most beautiful countryside in France.

3 The holiday _offers / consists of_ accommodation on a working farm.

4 You _have / are_ taught by expert local chefs.

5 You _can / need_ learn how to create delicious dishes.

6 You _can / must_ meet people with similar interests.

7 _Depart / Start_ any Saturday in August.

8 Book _quickly / early_ because places are limited.

4 Write sentences about an action and adventure tour of Costa Rica.

EXAMPLE
Action Costa Rica – perfect holiday for the adventure traveller
Action Costa Rica offers the perfect holiday for the adventure traveller.

1 Costa Rica – some of the world's most exciting landscapes

2 looked after by experienced guides

3 learn new skills

4 combine white-water rafting with mountain biking

5 taught by experts

6 book for the thrill of a lifetime

10 Communication

i Go to p.67 for instructions

✂

A Action and adventure

Bungee-jumping in New Zealand

Reasons in favour:

_____

_____

_____

_____

_____

_____

_____

_____

_____

_____

B Nature and ecology

Stay on a working farm in Spain

Reasons in favour:

_____

_____

_____

_____

_____

_____

_____

_____

_____

_____

C Culture and heritage

Tour the castles of Scotland and visit the Edinburgh
Arts Festival

Reasons in favour:

_____

_____

_____

_____

_____

_____

_____

_____

_____

_____

D Escape and enlightenment

Health spa in South Africa with meditation classes
and yoga

Reasons in favour:

_____

_____

_____

_____

_____

_____

_____

_____

_____

_____

11 Grammar test

1 Which four of these *if* clauses are correct?

1 If you fly to Paris …
2 If you will fly to Paris …
3 If you're flying to Paris …
4 If you have flown to Paris …
5 If you're going to fly to Paris …
6 If you would fly to Paris …

2 Which endings are possible in First Conditional sentences?

a you must have a ticket.
b could you do me a favour?
c you can get there before lunch.
d you'll get there quicker.
e you had to have a ticket.
f you might get there before lunch.
g you should ask for a window seat.
h you'll already know how quick it is.
i you would be there quicker.
j go with Air France – they have more flights.

3 Which of the four *if* clauses in **1** can go with the endings in **2**? There will usually be more than one possibility.

4 Put the verb forms in A in the correct place in the sentences in B. The verb forms are not in the right order.

A	B
1 can, meet, work	If you in a hotel you lots of people. = *If you* **work** *in a hotel, you* **can meet** *lots of people.*
2 can, stay, work	If you after midnight you in one of the guest rooms.
3 expect to, must, work, work	If you in a hotel you shifts.
4 ask, don't know, works	If you how something please your supervisor.
5 can't, come, must, phone	If you to work you before 8 a.m.
6 are, asked to, have to, wear, will, work	If you on the front desk you a uniform.

5 Make sentences beginning with *if*. Choose from the boxes.

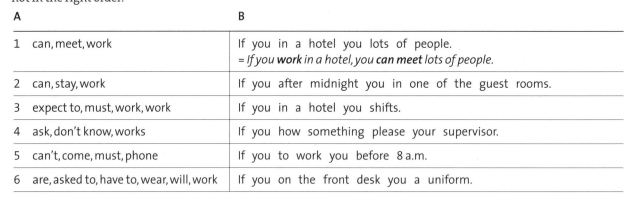

If	1 you lose your passport,	+	a he'll bring your suitcase to your room.
	2 you need a doctor,		b do you want to take out some insurance?
	3 you're travelling to the US,		c you must report it immediately.
	4 you tell the porter your room number,		d we cannot guarantee a ticket.
	5 you don't book in advance,		e call reception.
	6 you're worried about security,		f you may need a visa.

11 Communication

This is a race against time! You have to get the reservation data for journeys that your classmates are taking as quickly as possible.

1 Complete the information for yourself in the column below (you don't have to use real data).

	Example	You
From / to	London to New York	
Dates	15 Jan	
Flight number	AA006	
Departure time	11:00	
Arrival time	18:00	
Total cost	$325	
Credit card number	4417 8960 0072 1234	
Expiry date	05/2012	
Email address	pwallis@newhouse.com	
Contact phone no.	0774 362 486	

2 Stand up and move round the class as quickly as possible gathering the information on four other students and completing the blank chart. Make sure you get the information accurately, and that you give your information to others clearly. You MUST NOT show your data to the others.

	Passenger 1	Passenger 2	Passenger 3	Passenger 4
From / to				
Dates				
Flight number				
Departure time				
Arrival time				
Total cost				
Credit card number				
Expiry date				
Email address				
Contact phone no.				

3 When you have got the information for four passengers, shout *Stop!* as loudly as possible. Read the information back to the class – the four passengers must confirm that you have got it correctly. If not, the activity continues until the next person shouts '*Stop!*'

12 Grammar test

1 Put the sentences in this dialogue between a passenger and an airport official in the correct order.

a I'm waiting for them to announce the gate for the Atlanta flight. Can you find out what's happening?

b Oh no, sir. They're going to announce it in five minutes and there won't be a delay.

c Excuse me. I wonder if you could help me? *1*

d Yes, of course. The Atlanta flight? That's AA140.

e That's good. Thank you very much for your help.

f Certainly sir. How can I help?

g Yes, I think so. Do you know if there's a problem?

h You're welcome.

i Thank you. If you could.

j I'm sure there's no problem, sir. But let me just check for you.

k I see. Is that going to make it late?

l OK, I've checked. There was a problem loading the baggage.

2 Put the words in boxes in the correct order to make responses to the requests. Add punctuation and capital letters where necessary.

EXAMPLE

Could I ask you something?

| how – help – can I – certainly |

Certainly. How can I help?

1 Can we have a wheelchair for my mother?

| I'll – of course – wait here – get you one – and |

2 Could we get on an earlier flight?

| but – sorry – all the flights – I'm – are full |

3 Is it possible to have a seat with extra legroom?

| I'll – not sure – check – have to – I'm |

4 Can't you do things a bit quicker?

| have to – we – afraid – I'm – procedures – follow |

3 Complete the sentences said by airport officials for the following signs.

EXAMPLE Don't   *Don't smoke here!*

1 I'm sorry _____

2 If _____

3 Can _____

4 I'm sorry _____

5 Could _____

6 Don't _____

7 If _____

EXAMPLE

1

2

3

4

5

6

7

Swift Airlines

Name: **Mr Van Sassen**
Date: **August 12**
Flight: **AC094**
Depart: **Toronto 23:35h**
Arrive: **Buenos Aires 12:10h**
Price: **$3950.74**

12 Communication

i Go to p.67 for instructions

First Class

1A Name three jobs in air travel.

1B What is the difference between travel agents and tour operators?

1C Talk about three things you are good at.

1D What is the website of the national tourist office in your country?

2A Give three adjectives that can be used to describe beaches.

2B Think of three tourist destinations beginning with 'G'.

2C Describe the geographical features of a foreign country.

2D Describe places in your city where tourists can eat typical food.

3A What does *wholesaler* mean?

3B What are the four components of a package tour?

3C Use a time expression with each of these prepositions: *at*, *for*, *in*, *on*.

3D Name two tour operators based in your country.

Business Class

4A What does *VFR* stand for?

4B Name the three main categories used to describe reasons for travel.

4C Describe current trends in booking package holidays.

4D What are the main reasons why tourists visit your town or city?

5A Use the words *sell*, *sales*, and *sold* in three different sentences.

5B Name six services that a travel agency provides.

5C Give advice to a visitor to your town or city who likes art.

5D Suggest one way in which a local travel agent could improve business.

6A Name four types of land transport.

6B What is meant by a transport 'hub'?

6C Give three sentences comparing road and rail.

6D What's the best way to get around your country?

Economy Class

7A What are the four facilities you would most like in your hotel room?

7B What do you think the hotel of the future will be like?

7C You are the receptionist at a hotel. Answer the phone (in English!).

7D Which are the best and worst hotels in your town or city?

8A Give six alternatives for *nice*.

8B What is a SWOT analysis?

8C What's wrong with this sentence? *English is more easy than French.*

8D How can your local tourist authority improve the way they market your region?

9A Give three words that collocate with *flight*.

9B What's the difference between Ryanair and British Airways?

9C Describe two things that you like and two you don't like about air travel.

9D Name three airlines who operate in your country (and their codes).

10A What activities can you do with these animals: bird, horse, whale, camel?

10B What type of holidays will be popular in twenty years' time?

10C Ask three *Have you ever …?* questions.

10D Describe a 'holiday with a difference' in your country.

11A What are the nouns of these verbs: *reserve*, *confirm*, *cancel*?

11B Explain what CRS is.

11C Complete the sentence: *If you have a problem on your holiday …*

11D What CRS systems are used by travel agents in your town or city?

12A Give two words that collocate with *departure*.

12B List the stages from arriving at an airport to boarding the plane.

12C What would you say when a passenger crosses into a restricted zone?

12D What new facility would you like to introduce at your local airport?

1A	1B	1C	1D
2A	2B	2C	2D
3A	3B	3C	3D
4A	4B	4C	4D
5A	5B	5C	5D
6A	6B	6C	6D
7A	7B	7C	7D
8A	8B	8C	8D
9A	9B	9C	9D
10A	10B	10C	10D
11A	11B	11C	11D
12A	12B	12C	12D

Grammar tests key

Unit 1

1 1 wear a uniform.
2 to work as part of a team.
3 speaking on the telephone.
4 to use a computer.
5 to work long hours.
6 work (on) the night shift.
7 work at the hotel on the beach.

2 2 Are you able to work as part of a team?
3 Are you good at speaking on the telephone?
4 Do you know how to use a computer?
5 Are you willing to work long hours?

3 1 have to wear a uniform?
6 do you have to work (on) the night shift?
7 do you work at the hotel on the beach?

4 1 In the morning I usually work at the airport check-in desk, but this week I'm going to the gym.
2 For lunch I usually eat in the staff canteen, but this week I'm eating with friends or family.
3 In the afternoon I sometimes work in the departure lounge, but this week I'm going shopping.
4 In the evening I usually watch TV, but this week I'm going out with friends.
5 When I work I always go to bed at 10 p.m., but this week I'm going to bed at midnight.

Unit 2

1

1 is	6 is	11 are
2 is	7 is	12 has got
3 –	8 is	13 are
4 has got	9 has got	14 are
5 –	10 are	15 are

2 1 Where is Canada located?
2 What is the population of Canada?
3 What is the climate like?
4 What attractions are there?
5 Where are the cities located?
6 How many visitors are there every year?

3

Hi Julie

Well, here I am in Australia. We ~~stay~~ *are staying* in Sydney at the moment, which *is* located in the south-east. It's just great! There ~~is~~ *are* so many things to do. It's got nightclubs, restaurants, and there ~~is~~ *are* some fascinating tourist attractions. I took a group to the Sydney Harbour Bridge today, which is fantastic, because you can ~~enjoying~~ *enjoy* some great views. I've got a great group – they are enjoying the trip, and I think they ~~are liking~~ *like* me as well. Tomorrow we're flying to Alice Springs and then to Ayers Rock, which ~~is lying~~ *lies* in the centre of Australia. The weather ~~are~~ *is* very hot there. You can ~~to~~ *do* so much in this wonderful country. Our brochure is right: Australia ~~offer~~ *offers* everything under the sun!

Bye

Angela

Unit 3

1 **Possible answers**

1 What do you specialize in?
2 What type of tours do you offer?
3 Are they only available to young people?
4 What's included in the price?
5 What type of hotels do you use?
6 What is the commission rate?

2

at	for	in
Christmas	a long time	2008
the weekend	two weeks	the winter
6 a.m.	three years	the evening
10 o'clock		a year's time
breakfast		
13.00		

on	(no preposition)
Saturday	today
14 August	next week
my birthday	this afternoon
	yesterday

3 1 Does the tour only leave ~~in~~ *on* Friday?

2 Is it true the tour lasts ~~on~~ *for* six days?

3 When ~~arrives~~ *does* the coach *arrive* at the hotel in Vilnius?

4 What time *do* they serve dinner?

5 We leave the hotel in Vilnius in the morning ~~on~~ *at* 8 a.m. Is that correct?

6 How long *does* it ~~takes~~ *take* from Vilnius to Riga?

7 What time ~~on~~ *in* the afternoon do we check in to the hotel in Riga?

8 Does the tour operate ~~on~~ *in* winter as well as summer?

9 Is there a special tour ~~in~~ *at* Christmas?

10 Do your prices increase ~~in~~ next year?

Unit 4

1 1 d To get into the country.

2 f Because it's not allowed.

3 i For a security check.

4 b In case there's an emergency.

5 e Because of a staff shortage.

6 a Because it's full.

7 j To check you're in the right seat.

8 c For pleasure.

9 h In case you get lost and need to phone me.

10 g Because of a delay in loading the baggage.

Question 8 is not asked by a traveller.

2 1 The graph shows that the number of international arrivals <u>has risen dramatically</u> since 1950.

2 From 1950 to 1960 the number of international tourist arrivals <u>grew steadily</u> from 30 million to 80 million.

3 Between 1950 and 2000 the figure <u>increased sharply</u> by nearly 28-fold.

4 In the present day the number of arrivals <u>is continuing</u> to grow <u>dramatically</u>.

5 By 2020 the figure <u>will be</u> 1580 million.

Unit 5

1 Possible answers

1 What's your phone number?

2 Have you booked with us before?

3 Do you want to go to Cyprus again?

4 What type of holiday are you looking for?

5 Do you know when you want to go?

6 How long do you want to stay?

7 How many of you are in the party?

8 What type of accommodation are you looking for?

2 Possible answers

1 Why don't you go for a weekend break in Prague?

2 How about going for a week in a farmhouse in the French countryside?

3 If I were you, I'd go for a one month 'Inter-rail' holiday travelling around Europe by train.

4 Have you thought of going for a weekend in a five-star hotel in New York?

5 Your best option is to go for an adventure holiday trekking in the Himalayas.

Unit 6

1 1 more complicated than

2 more expensive than

3 shorter

4 more luxurious

5 better than

6 more interesting

7 as exciting as

8 as comfortable as

9 more romantic than

10 easier than

11 busier

2 1 No, it doesn't. It arrives at 7.40.

2 No, it isn't. It's five days a week.

3 No, they're not. They're every three hours.

4 No, it doesn't. It leaves at 7.10 p.m.

5 Yes, you can – subject to space availability.

6 Yes, there are – for seniors.

Unit 7

1 1 within

2 from

3 within

4 from

5 near

6 in

7 near / next to

8 in

9 between

10 opposite / next to

11 behind

12 in the heart of

2 **Possible answers**

1 What type of room would you like?

2 When would you want to stay?

3 How would you like to pay?

4 What's the name on the card?

5 How do you spell the last name?

6 What's the expiry date?

3 **Possible answers**

As you enter the hotel you will find the Reception on your right. Behind the reception desk are administration offices. On the left hand side as you enter there ~~is a large office~~ *is a shop* and next to ~~it~~ *them*, a little further on, ~~a smaller office~~ *a gym*. Just beyond this, after a small doorway that leads to ~~the indoor and outdoor gardens~~ *the outdoor swimming pool and sauna*, and the car park, is ~~another office~~ *the Internet room*. Opposite the main entrance are the lifts and stairs that will take you to the guest rooms. As you stand at the reception desk and look to your left, you will see the ~~restaurant~~ *conference room* and behind, a little further down the corridor, is the ~~bar~~ *restaurant*.

Unit 8

1 1 geared

2 hoping to

3 gear

4 to / towards

5 let

6 hope

7 let

2 1 oldest

2 cheapest

3 newest

4 most beautiful

5 biggest

6 most expensive

7 smallest

3 1 most historic

2 most economical

3 most modern

4 most gorgeous

5 largest

6 most luxurious

7 tiniest

4 1 Let us ~~to~~ help you relax, Caribbean-style.

2 For one of the most exciting experiences of *your* life, come to China.

3 Book with e-line: nothing could be ~~more easy~~ *easier*.

4 Tom's taxis: we're geared *to* meeting your needs.

5 Stay at the most ~~luxury~~ luxurious hotel on the Costa Brava.

6 Hire the Minimax – the ~~bigest~~ *biggest* small car on the market.

Unit 9

1 1 I love working with great colleagues.

2 I like staying in nice hotels.

3 I quite like giving the safety demonstration.

4 I don't mind wearing a uniform.

5 I don't like serving food.

6 I really don't like working on long-haul flights.

7 I hate spending time away from my boyfriend.

8 I really hate dealing with difficult passengers.

2 Possible answers

Questionnaire	Direct question	Indirect question
1 Age?	*How old are you?*	*Would you mind telling me how old you are?*
2 Travelling alone?	*Are you travelling alone?*	*Could you tell me if you are travelling alone?*
3 Occupation?	What's your job / occupation?	Can you tell me your job / occupation?
4 Destination?	Where are you going?	Would you mind telling me where you are going?
5 Reason for journey?	What's the reason for your journey?	Could you tell me the reason for your journey?
6 Airline?	Which airline are you flying with?	Can I ask you which airline you are flying with?
7 Length of flight?	How long is the flight?	Would you mind telling me how long the flight is?
8 First time with this airline?	Is this your first time with this airline?	Could you tell me if this is your first time with this airline?
9 Frequent flyer?	Are you a frequent flyer? Or: Have you flown many times before?	Can I ask you if you are a frequent flyer? Or: Can I ask you if you have flown many times before?
10 Like flying in general?	Do you like flying?	Would you mind telling me if you like flying?
11 Join our Frequent Flyer Programme?	Would you like to join our Frequent Flyer Programme?	Could you tell me if you would like to join our Frequent Flyer Programme?
12 Give me your email address?	What's your email address?	Can I ask you what your email address is?

3 1 d, 2 e, 3 f, 4 c, 5 b, 6 a

Unit 10

1 1 started
2 was
3 has grown
4 went
5 have included
6 have had
7 visited

2 A Have you ever been water-skiing?
B No, I haven't.
A Have you ever been windsurfing?
B Yes, I have.
A When did you go?
B Last year. (or: I went last year.)
A Where did you go?
B Greece. (or: I went to Greece.)
A Did you like it?
B Yes, I did.

3 1 is
2 boasts
3 offers
4 are
5 can
6 can
7 Depart
8 early

4 1 Costa Rica boasts some of the world's most exciting landscapes.
2 You are looked after by experienced guides.
3 You can learn new skills.
4 You can combine white-water rafting with mountain biking.
5 You are taught by experts.
6 Book early (or now) for the thrill of a lifetime.

Unit 11

1 1, 3, 4, 5

2 a, b, c, d, f, g, h, j

3 1, 3, and 5: a, b, c, d, f, g, j
4 h

4 2 If you **work** after midnight, you **can stay** in one of the guest rooms.

3 If you **work** in a hotel, you **must expect to work** shifts.

4 If you **don't know** how something **works**, please **ask** your supervisor.

5 If you **can't come** to work, you **must phone** before 8 a.m.

6 If you **are asked to work** on the front desk, you **will have to wear** a uniform.

5 1 c, 2 e, 3 f, 4 a, 5 d, 6 b

Unit 12

1 1 c, 2 f, 3 a, 4 d, 5 g, 6 j, 7 i, 8 l,
9 k, 10 b, 11 e, 12 h

2 1 Of course. Wait here and I'll get you one.

2 I'm sorry, but all the flights are full.

3 I'm not sure. I'll have to check.

4 I'm afraid we have to follow procedures.

3 **Possible answers**

1 I'm sorry, but can you take off your shoes?

2 If you have a luggage trolley, you must leave it here.

3 Can you turn off your mobile phone, please?

4 I'm sorry, but you can't use your laptop.

5 Could you stand behind the line, please?

6 Don't bring any food or drink.

7 If you don't have a ticket, you can't enter.